AQA
GCSE

WORKING WITH THE ANTHOLOGY
chieve a C

Childs
hly experienced Chief Examiner

www.pearsonschoolsandfecolleges.co.uk

✓ Free online support
✓ Useful weblinks
✓ 24 hour online ordering

0845 630 33 33

Part of Pearson

Contents

Introduction

How does this book work?

This book is designed to help students raise their achievement in Unit 2 or Unit 5 of the AQA GCSE English Literature specification. It is tailored to the requirements of the specification to help students achieve grades E–B.

The book breaks the Assessment Objectives down into their component parts. It then provides students with:

▶ guidance and teaching on the key skills that make the difference between an E, D, C and B grade

▶ examples of students' work at grades E, D, C and B with examiner comments which highlight what is good and what could be improved

▶ activities that allow them to reflect on and improve their learning

▶ the relevant mark scheme descriptors together with guidance on what the examiners are looking for

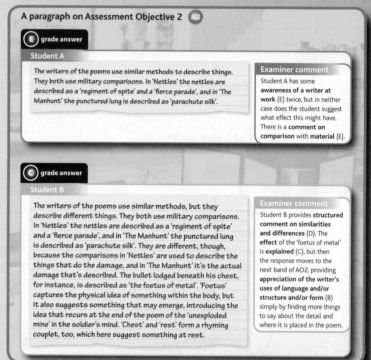

A paragraph on Assessment Objective 2 AO2

E grade answer

Student A

The writers of the poems use similar methods to describe things. They both use military comparisons. In 'Nettles' the nettles are described as a 'regiment of spite' and a 'fierce parade', and in 'The Manhunt' the punctured lung is described as 'parachute silk'.

Examiner comment

Student A has some **awareness of a writer at work** (E) twice, but in neither case does the student suggest what effect this might have. There is a **comment on comparison** with **material** (E).

grade answer

Student B

The writers of the poems use similar methods, but they describe different things. They both use military comparisons. In 'Nettles' the nettles are described as a 'regiment of spite' and a 'fierce parade', and in 'The Manhunt' the punctured lung is described as 'parachute silk'. They are different, though, because the comparisons in 'Nettles' are used to describe the things that do the damage, and in 'The Manhunt' it's the actual damage that's described. The bullet lodged beneath his chest, for instance, is described as 'the foetus of metal'. 'Foetus' captures the physical idea of something within the body, but it also suggests something that may emerge, introducing the idea that recurs at the end of the poem of the 'unexploded mine' in the soldier's mind. 'Chest' and 'rest' form a rhyming couplet, too, which here suggest something at rest.

Examiner comment

Student B provides **structured comment on similarities and differences** (D). The **effect** of the 'foetus of metal' is **explained** (C), but then the response moves to the next band of AO2, providing **appreciation of the writer's uses of language and/or structure and/or form** (B) simply by finding more things to say about the detail and where it is placed in the poem.

▶ hints from an experienced Chief Examiner on how to move up the grades.

The approach that this book uses comes from many years of examining experience and out of workshops, training sessions and revision courses with teachers and students. It can be used with confidence by all students who have the potential to move from a grade E or D, to a C, and then to a B.

How is the book structured?

The book is broken down into 6 Chapters. Chapters 1–4 cover the poems in the AQA Anthology and the following approach is taken in each of these chapters:

▶ Looking at the poems as a whole.
▶ Looking at the poems individually.
▶ Comparing the poems and writing in the exam.

Each chapter also includes:

▶ an explanation of the relevant Assessment Objectives
▶ learning objectives ('My learning')
▶ activities
▶ glossed words from the poems
▶ contextual explanations
▶ sample answers with examiner comments
▶ opportunities for peer or self-assessment.

Chapter 5 focuses on the Unseen poem and Chapter 6 provides a complete practice exam paper together with mark schemes and explanations.

What do the Assessment Objectives mean?

AO1: in response to the first Assessment Objective you must write about your response to the poems using details from the poems to support your ideas. You can say what you think the poem is about as a whole or what particular details mean, and you should think about how other readers might interpret these details.

AO2: in response to the second Assessment Objective you have to write about the writers' methods and their purposes in using these methods. The methods are broken down into three:

▶ **Language:** the words the writers have chosen to use, their vocabulary, their use of imagery, and so on.
▶ **Structure:** the way the writers have chosen to order their words and ideas either within a whole poem (what have the writers chosen to begin and end the poem with?) or within a stanza or sometimes even within a single line.
▶ **Form:** the particular form of poetry chosen. It can refer to the overall structure chosen, such as sonnet form, or details the writer has chosen, such as rhyme and rhythm.

Although you need to think about all of these things when you work on a poem, you won't necessarily have to write about all of them in the exam. For instance, in the C descriptor **explanation of writers' uses of language and/or structure and/or form**, 'and/or' means just that – so an explanation of language would be enough. However, you must always use details from the poems to support what you are saying and link the technique you're writing about to the meaning you think the writer was trying to convey or its effect on the reader.

AO3: in response to the third Assessment Objective you have to compare both what the poems are about and the ways in which they are written, using details from the poems to support your ideas.

The AQA GCSE English Literature specification

This book is for students taking Unit 2 or Unit 5 of the AQA GCSE English Literature specification. Unit 2 offers students the opportunity to be assessed on the poetry requirements in an exam. Unit 5 offers the poetry assessment as Controlled Assessment. The principal focus of this book is on Unit 2. However, students taking Unit 5 will find most of the content of this book relevant and helpful.

An overview of the full GCSE specification for English Literature, including the requirements for Unit 5, can be found in the corresponding Heinemann Teacher Guide or on the AQA website.

GCSE English Literature Unit 2

Here is an overview of the Unit 2 exam. This book is principally designed to support this unit.

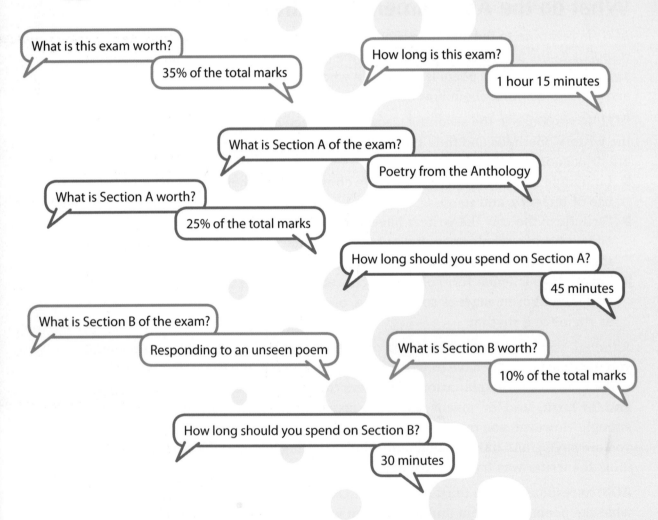

What is this exam worth?

35% of the total marks

How long is this exam?

1 hour 15 minutes

What is Section A of the exam?

Poetry from the Anthology

What is Section A worth?

25% of the total marks

How long should you spend on Section A?

45 minutes

What is Section B of the exam?

Responding to an unseen poem

What is Section B worth?

10% of the total marks

How long should you spend on Section B?

30 minutes

For full details, see the corresponding Teacher Guide and AQA specification.

AQA GCSE English Literature: further resources from Pearson Education

▶ Teacher Guide – full colour 'visual' lesson plans can be found in the corresponding Heinemann Teacher Guide, written by experienced author and Head of English, David Grant. These lesson plans also make suggestions about how to incorporate materials from the AQA Digital Anthology. Full support for the Controlled Assessment requirements is also included, written by Peter Thomas.

▶ Heinemann and Longman set texts – the AQA specification prescribes Heinemann and Longman editions of several set texts. For details of the widest available range of hardback educational editions, see our website or catalogue.

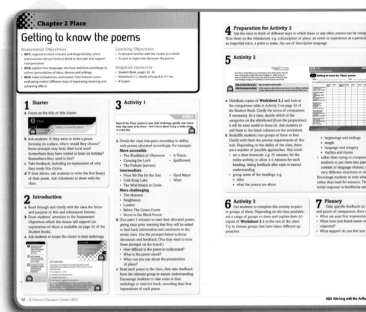

▶ Heinemann ActiveTeach for *Of Mice and Men* and *An Inspector Calls* – exciting new ActiveTeach versions of the two most popular set texts, available as educational e-books exclusively from Pearson Education. In addition to an electronic copy of the text that corresponds to our educational edition you will find a wealth of resources to help students engage with and understand the text, as well as a bank of activities focused on grade improvement.

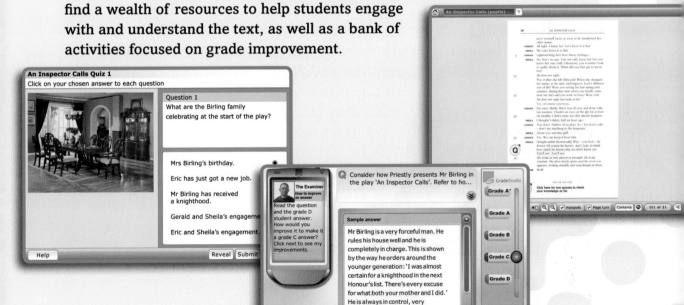

In this section you will learn how to:
- become familiar with the poems as a whole
- start to make links between the poems.

Assessment Objectives:

 AO1 respond to texts critically and imaginatively; select and evaluate relevant textual detail to illustrate and support interpretations.

 AO2 explain how language, structure and form contribute to writers' presentation of ideas, themes and settings.

 AO3 make comparisons and explain links between texts, evaluating writers' different ways of expressing meaning and achieving effects.

Getting to know the poems

The poems

The Clown Punk
Simon Armitage

Checking Out Me History
John Agard

Horse Whisperer
Andrew Forster

Medusa
Carol Ann Duffy

Singh Song
Daljit Nagra

Brendon Gallacher
Jackie Kay

Give
Simon Armitage

Les Grands Seigneurs
Dorothy Molloy

Ozymandias
Percy Bysshe Shelley

My Last Duchess
Robert Browning

The River God
Stevie Smith

The Hunchback in the Park
Dylan Thomas

The Ruined Maid
Thomas Hardy

Casehistory: Alison (head injury)
U. A. Fanthorpe

On a Portrait of a Deaf Man
John Betjeman

Introduction

The poems in this chapter focus on character and voice. Learning how a poet uses character and voice is a key part of enjoying and analysing poetry. All the poems are in your AQA Anthology.

In this chapter you will be:

▶ looking at the individual poems

▶ comparing the poems

▶ learning how to approach exam questions.

This preparation will help you develop your writing skills in order to hit the Assessment Objectives.

See page v for more information about what the Assessment Objectives mean. In the exam you will have to compare two poems from this chapter.

Getting started

The first thing to do is to start to get to know the 'Character and voice' poems.

ACTIVITY 1

Read all the 'Character and voice' poems in your AQA Anthology. Just notice what they seem to be about – don't worry about trying to make sense of every line.

ACTIVITY 2

Write the headings listed below on a sheet of paper. Under each heading make notes of any links between poems. Include poems that have similarities and differences. Use the tips below to help you.

Headings	Tips
What the poems are about	Poems might be about death, birth, memory, relationship between parent and child. Make a note of poems that seem to have some meanings or ideas in common.
Beginnings/endings	Find examples of lines that look similar, but where there's a difference too. For example, both 'Medusa' and 'Casehistory: Alison' end with single lines, separated from the rest of the poem, but they have very different effects on the reader.
Length	You might notice some distinct similarities or differences. Include the number and length of **stanzas**, if there are any.
Rhyme	Is there a regular **rhyme scheme**? Does it change? Be careful – some poems that don't seem to rhyme often use a lot of **half-rhyme** or **echoes**, or might suddenly rhyme. Look at 'The Clown Punk', for example. There are a lot of half-rhymes, but only one full rhyme, in the last two lines. If you were working on this poem, you'd need to think about why the writer does this.
Rhythm	'Checking Out Me History' is one poem that has a strong **rhythm**. Can you find others?
Language	Some poems are older than others, and some might use non-standard forms of English. Look for ones that are similar, and ones that are very different. For example, 'The Ruined Maid' uses some nineteenth-century rural English, whereas 'Checking Out Me History' uses Caribbean English.
Imagery	Some poems are rich in **imagery** such as **metaphors** and **similes**, whereas others might seem quite plain. Make a note of some obvious similarities and differences.

Now display your findings on a sheet of A3 paper in one of the following ways.

1   Spread the titles out on the sheet and draw links between them, labelling each one.

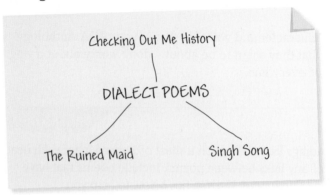

Checking Out Me History

DIALECT POEMS

The Ruined Maid   Singh Song

2   Draw a picture or symbol for each idea (such as death or nature) that appears in more than one poem, and group the poems around each – a poem can appear in more than one group.

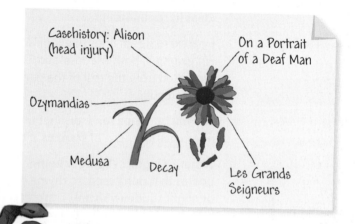

Casehistory: Alison (head injury)

On a Portrait of a Deaf Man

Ozymandias

Medusa   Decay

Les Grands Seigneurs

3   Draw a picture, or pictures, for each poem on the sheet, and link similar ones with arrows.

In these activities you have started to tackle all three Assessment Objectives. Now you will be focusing on AO1 and AO2 as you look at the poems individually (pages 5–21). You will return to AO3 when you compare the poems (pages 22–25). Finally, you will look at how to turn your knowledge and skills into successful exam answers, before you attempt one yourself (pages 26–33).

Looking at the poems individually

Looking at the poems individually

My learning ▶

In this section you will learn how to:
- develop your responses to the poems
- relate the Assessment Objectives to the poems.

This section of the chapter, pages 5–21, will lead you through each individual poem. Throughout, you will find examples of student responses at different levels.

In the exam, you will have to write about the poems individually. You will also have to compare two poems; one named poem and one unnamed, which means you can choose the second one.

Assessment Objectives:

The Assessment Objectives you will be focusing on in this part of the chapter are:

 A01 respond to texts critically and imaginatively; select and evaluate relevant textual detail to illustrate and support interpretations.

 A02 explain how language, structure and form contribute to writers' presentation of ideas, themes and settings.

The Clown Punk
by Simon Armitage

Read the poem in your AQA Anthology, then complete the activities below.

▶**Poem Glossary**

shonky dirty, derelict

Initial responses

ACTIVITY 1

1   The poem is about a man who Armitage calls the clown punk. Why do you think he has given him this name?

2   The **speaker** describes a time when the clown punk 'slathers his daft mush on the windscreen'. Explain what he did in your own words.

3   What details tell you that the clown punk is poor?

4   Armitage compares the clown punk to 'a basket of washing that got up and walked'. What does this suggest about his appearance?

5   Why might the children 'wince and scream' at the clown punk?

6   What will happen to the clown punk when he gets older?

7   There are a lot of references to colour in the poem. Find one, and decide what the colour makes you think about the clown.

8   What do you think the writer wants you to feel about the clown punk at the end of the poem? For example, does he want you to laugh at him? Feel sorry for him? Be scared of him? Write a sentence or two explaining your answer.

Words/phrases to explore (AO1 and AO2)

ACTIVITY 2

1   Write down all the words you can find in the poem which Armitage uses to describe the clown punk, such as 'a basket of washing' and 'deflated'. What do all the words you have found suggest about the speaker's attitude to the clown punk?

2   Think carefully about the phrase 'let it rain' at the end of the poem. What do you think the speaker means? Try to think of two or three different possible answers.

Checking Out Me History

by John Agard

Read the poem in your AQA Anthology, then complete the activities below.

Initial responses

1   This poem is about the history that people are taught, and other history that we might not know about.
    Find examples in the poem of the following things that people do learn in school:
    *   real events
    *   characters from children's stories
    *   nursery **rhymes**.

2   'Dem never tell me bout dat'. Which people and events has the **speaker** not been told about?

3   Look at the **stanzas** about Toussaint, Nanny and Mary Seacole.
    a   Pick out all the words that suggest the speaker admires the characters, for example 'beacon'. Write these words down.
    b   Why do you think the writer has chosen to use short lines in those stanzas, when the others have much longer lines? Think about the effect of the short lines.

4   Look at the stanza about Nanny.
    a   Some words, such as 'see-far woman', suggest Nanny is almost an unreal figure, rather than human. Which other words suggest this?
    b   Which words suggest something real?
    c   Why do you think the writer refers to her as a 'fire-woman' and compares her to a 'stream' and a 'river'?

5   At the end of the poem, what does the speaker decide he has to do?

Words/phrases to explore (AO1 and AO2)

Agard begins the poem with 'Dem tell me', and repeats it at the beginning of the last stanza. Who are 'dem' by the end of the poem, do you think?

Contexts

Toussaint L'Ouverture was a Haitian revolutionary leader. Born a slave, he was credited with establishing Haiti's independence.
Nanny de Maroon was the spiritual leader of the Windward Maroons. She directed an effective resistance movement against the British.
Shaka was a great leader of the Zulu people in South Africa.
The Caribs and Arawaks were among the Caribbean people whose islands were taken over after the Europeans arrived in 1492.
Mary Seacole was a nurse who helped wounded and dying British soldiers in the Crimean war.

Sample answer C

To achieve a C on this AO2 descriptor, you need to show **explanation of effects of writer's use of language.** To do this, you need to explain clearly what the effect is on you as the reader, not just say what the device is. The following extract from a sample answer would hit the grade C requirement.

> Activity 1, question 3a
> The writer describes Mary Seacole as 'a healing star' and 'a yellow sunrise'. These metaphors suggest something high in the sky, and shining, so she's like a hero, somebody to look up to, as the speaker clearly does.

Horse Whisperer

by Andrew Forster

Read the poem in your AQA Anthology, then complete the activities below.

GradeStudio

Sample answer ©

To achieve a C on this AO2 descriptor, you need to show **explanation of effect(s) of writer's uses of language and/ or structure and/or form**. The following extract from a sample answer would hit the grade C requirement.

> **Activity 1, question 7**
>
> 'Stampede' is quite a normal word to use to describe the hasty exit of a lot of people, but in this poem 'stampede' makes you think of the horses, because really it applies to animals – so it seems as though the whisperers were driven out like the animals they treated.

Initial responses

ACTIVITY 1

1. What different things does the whisperer do to help the horses, or the people who owned them?

2. **a** Make a list of the things the speaker says and thinks about horses.
   b For each item in your list, write down what this shows about her attitude to horses.

3. How does the speaker see herself? What sort of character does she think she is? Look at what she says about herself, and the words she uses to describe what she does.

4. Why do you think the whisperer's 'secret' in the first **stanza** worked? Why would it draw the horses to her?

5. What was the 'legacy of whispers' do you think?

6. The first two stanzas describe how people used to want the whisperer, because 'They shouted for me'. What changed this? Look in the third stanza for the clue. Why do you think it led to the whisperers being driven out?

7. Which word in the fourth stanza suggests that the whisperer is almost like the horses?

Words/phrases to explore (AO1 and AO2)

ACTIVITY 2

Look at the end of the poem.

1. How does the writer create a sense of the horses being alive by the words he uses here? Look at the type of words he uses and the repetition of sound and **rhythm**.

2. Why would the whisperer know about the breath and veins? Think about where she would stand.

Medusa

by Carol Ann Duffy

Read the poem in
your AQA Anthology,
then complete the
activities below.

GradeStudio

Context

Medusa In Greek mythology
Medusa was a Gorgon, a creature
whose gaze turned onlookers to
stone. She was the only mortal
Gorgon, and the goddess Athena
turned Medusa's hair into snakes
when she found her lying in her
temple with Poseidon. She was
killed by Perseus, who avoided her
gaze by looking at her in a mirror
rather than directly.

Initial responses

ACTIVITY 1

1   What does Medusa suspect about her husband, and what does
    she try to do to him?

2   Carol Ann Duffy takes the story of Medusa and imagines her as an
    ageing woman. What references to the Greek myth described above
    can you find in the poem?

3   a   In the first **stanza**, what is it that turns her hair into snakes?
    b   How does Duffy make her thoughts seem like snakes? Look for
        words that you might associate with snakes.

4   In the second stanza, how does Duffy makes the woman seem
    ageing? Think about what the words suggest as well as what they say
    directly.

5   In the same stanza, the writer makes the woman seem dangerous.
    How?

6   Why should the man be 'terrified' that Medusa loves him?

7   Look at the end of the poem.
    a   What words and phrases are repeated? What do they tell you
        about Medusa's state of mind?
    b   Why do you think Duffy places the last sentence on a separate
        line? Think about the effect this has.
    c   Why do you think Medusa wants the man to look at her? Think of
        more than one reason.

GradeStudio

Sample answer B

To achieve a B on this AO2
descriptor, you need to show
**appreciation/consideration
of writers' uses of language
and/or structure and/or form
and effects on readers**. To do
this, you need to say at least two
things about a writer's choice. The
following extract from a sample
answer would hit the grade B
requirement.

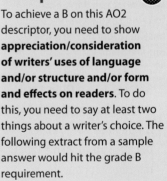

Activity 1, question 7b
The last line being on
its own makes the threat
seem immediate, and the
last word 'now' makes
the reader imagine the
end of the poem is the
moment when he turns
to stone.

Words/phrases to explore (AO1)

ACTIVITY 2

Which phrase in the poem best sums up Medusa's state of mind?
Make sure that you can find more than one reason for your choice.

Singh Song

by Daljit Nagra

Read the poem in your AQA Anthology, then complete the activities below.

GradeStudio

Sample answer D

To achieve a D on this AO2 descriptor, you need to show **explained response to element(s) of text**. This means you need to explain why you think what you think. The following extract from a sample answer would hit the grade D requirement.

> **Activity 1, question 1**
> I think Singh must be a hopeless shopkeeper, because he doesn't label his goods properly, his shop is dirty, and he closes when he feels like it to be with his horrible bride.

Initial responses

ACTIVITY 1

1   Although there are other voices in the poem, the main voice is Singh's. What does the poem reveal about his life? Think about:
    • what he has to do   • how he is treated by other people.

2   What is revealed about Singh's character? Think about:
    • his response to other people   • his attitude to his bride.

3   What is revealed about Singh's bride? Think about:
    • what she does   • her appearance   • her attitude to other people.

4   Look at the **stanza** beginning 'Late in de midnight hour'. Which words and phrases suggest an atmosphere of romance here, and which words and phrases seem to show the opposite?

5   Look at the conversation between Singh and his bride. How are their words typical of each of them?

6   The last line of the poem is 'Is priceless baby'. Can you think of more than one meaning for the word 'priceless' here? Why do you think the writer decided to end with this word?

7   The voice in the poem speaks in Indian English. Which words do you think are **dialect words** (words from a specific region), rather than the writer just showing accent (how the words are spoken)?

Words/phrases to explore (AO1)

ACTIVITY 2

What do you think are the most important things in Singh's life, and what doesn't he care about? Write these in a list, using details from the poem. Then turn your list into a paragraph of writing to answer the question.

Brendon Gallacher

by Jackie Kay

Read the poem in your AQA Anthology, then complete the activities below.

Initial responses

ACTIVITY 1

1   'My Brendon Gallacher' is repeated throughout the poem. Why do you think the writer includes it three times in the opening **stanza**?

2   In the first stanza the writer creates a contrast between the **speaker's** family and Brendon's by balancing the two as she writes. The first is 'He was seven and I was six.' Write down as many other balances like this from the first stanza as you can.

3   What clue does the first line of the second stanza give for another possible reason for the child inventing Brendon? What does that tell you about the child's life?

4   'how his mum drank and his daddy was a cat burglar.' Why do you think the child creates this?

5   a   What additional things about Brendon that might appeal to the speaker are mentioned in the last stanza?
    b   Do they suggest anything about the child?

6   a   Why do you think the writer repeats the words 'oh' and 'Brendon' in the last line?
    b   What does this repetition tell you about how the child is feeling?

Words/phrases to explore (AO2)

ACTIVITY 2

The line 'how his mum drank and his daddy was a cat burglar' sounds like a child speaking. How does the writer create the language and thoughts of a child? Look for simple words and sentences.

GradeStudio

Sample answer

To achieve a C on this AO2 descriptor, you need to show **appropriate comment on ideas/ themes**. The following extract from a sample answer would hit the grade C requirement.

'And he died then' is a moment of shock for the reader – not only the realisation that Brendon was an 'imaginary friend', but that he was a friend so real as to be living for the child. The loss is very real for her, therefore.

GradeStudio

GradeStudio

Context

Gold, **frankincense** and **myrrh** were the gifts that the three wise men brought to the infant Jesus, according to the Bible.

GradeStudio

Sample answer ⊙

To achieve a C on this AO2 descriptor, you need to show **appropriate comment on ideas/themes.** To do this, you need to make a clear statement about an idea in the poem. The following extract from a sample answer would hit the grade C requirement:

> **Activity 1, question 5**
> The beggar doesn't like his situation, and seems resentful – he's made a deliberate choice of of the person to approach, and 'That's big of you' seems almost aggressive.

Give

by Simon Armitage

Read the poem in your AQA Anthology, then complete the activities below.

Initial responses

ACTIVITY 1

1 What is the **speaker's** situation, exactly? Why do you think he is desperate?

2 Who do you think the beggar is speaking to? Try to think of more than one possibility, and then check through the poem to see if the beggar's words make sense for each possibility.

3 What does the other person think of the beggar? Find a detail from the poem to back up your point.

4 How does the beggar feel about having to beg? How do you know?

5 How does the reader know that the beggar is desperate? Look at the middle of the poem, not just the end, and trace the way the voice moves from one thing to the next.

6 a There are lots of patterns in this poem. Look at the first two lines, which form a sentence, and the next two lines, which also form a sentence. How are they very alike in the words the writer has chosen?
  b The sentences end with the two words 'here' and 'yours'. Why do you think the writer has decided to end with these?
  c How does **rhyme** emphasise these two words?

7 Now look at the last two lines.
  a What do you notice about the length of sentences?
  b Is there any rhyme or **half-rhyme** in these lines?
  c What is the effect of these last two lines?

ACTIVITY 2

Words/phrases to explore (A01)

Look again at line 10. What 'change' does the speaker mean?
Think about two possible meanings for the word.

Les Grands Seigneurs

by Dorothy Molloy

Read the poem in your AQA Anthology, then complete the activities below.

Initial responses

ACTIVITY 1

1 In the first three **stanzas**, what is the relationship between the **speaker** and the men she knew? Think about who was in charge.

2 In the first two stanzas, the speaker makes fourteen comparisons with men. The first two lines contain comparisons to features of buildings, such as towers. There are three more types of things that the speaker uses. Decide what they are.

3 In the third stanza the speaker thinks about herself.
  a In the first line and a half, how does she see the relationship which she used to have with men?
  b She says that they 'played at courtly love'. Look back at the first two stanzas. What items does she mention that belong to past times rather than modern times?

4 The last stanza changes everything.
  a Which word in the first line shows that things have changed?
  b How is the language of the stanza now modern instead of old? Write down any examples of words that sound modern rather than old.
  c Look at the list of things that she 'became'. What do all of these things tell you about the relationship now?
  d Why does the change happen 'overnight', do you think?

Words/phrases to explore (AO1)

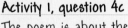
ACTIVITY 2

Look again at the last word of the poem. What do you think the speaker means by her 'bluff'?

GradeStudio

Sample answer ⒟

To achieve a D on this AO1 descriptor, you need to show **awareness of ideas/themes**. The following extract from a sample answer would hit the grade D requirement.

> Activity 1, question 4c
> The poem is about the relationship between women and men, and how it changes once a woman is married: the woman suddenly becomes a 'plaything' rather than what she was to the man before.

To move to **appropriate comment** (C), the comment would have to be extended, and be more exact about the change.

Context

Ozymandias was another name for Rameses, one of the Egyptian pharaohs.

Sample answer 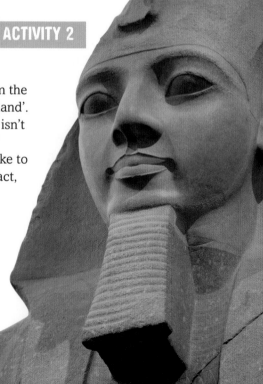C

To achieve a C on this AO2 descriptor, you need to show **explanation of effect(s) of writers' uses of language and/or structure and/or form and effects on readers**. The following extract from a sample answer would hit the grade C requirement because it explains the effect of the use of certain words.

Activity 1, question 7
In the last line the words 'level' and 'stretch far away' emphasise how complete the destruction is, because it suggests that absolutely nothing is breaking the surface of the sand, where there used to be a great civilisation.

Ozymandias

by Percy Bysshe Shelley

Read the poem in your AQA Anthology, then complete the activities below.

Initial responses

ACTIVITY 1

1 Ozymandias was a great king. What tells you this in the poem?

2 Find and write down the **adjectives** in lines 2 and 4. What picture do they create of the statue?

3 What do the ends of line 4 and line 5 suggest about the nature of the king?

4 How do you think the king treated his subjects? Try to find a detail to support your view.

5 a 'Look on my works, Ye Mighty, and despair!' What did Ozymandias mean when he had this written on his statue?
   b What does it mean now that the statue has been destroyed?

6 Line 12 begins 'Nothing beside remains.' This is the shortest sentence in the poem.
   a Why do you think Shelley has used such a short sentence?
   b Why do you think he has placed it after the previous thought, 'Look on my works, Ye Mighty, and despair!'?

7 Find the adjectives in the last two lines. What do they emphasise?

Words/phrases to explore (AO1 and AO2)

ACTIVITY 2

1 At the beginning of the poem the traveller is 'from an antique land'. Why do you think the writer isn't more exact about the place?

2 What difference would it make to the poem if he was more exact, and made it about a specific place?

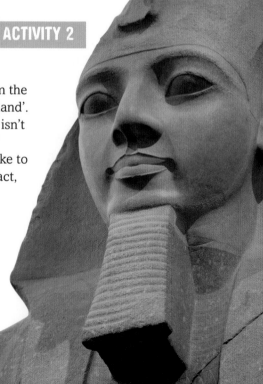

My Last Duchess

by Robert Browning

Read the poem in your AQA Anthology, then complete the activities below.

▶ **Poem Glossary**

lessoned taught, insructed

forsooth indeed

Neptune the Roman god of the sea

GradeStudio

Contexts

Ferrara a duchy in northern Italy. The Duke is probably based on Alfonso, who was duke of Ferrara from 1559 to 1597, and whose wife Lucrezia died in 1561 at the age of 17.
Frà Pandolf/Claus of Innsbruck these two artists are probably fictional.

Initial responses

ACTIVITY 1

1   What is your first impression of the Duke? Find some details from the poem to support what you think.

2   This poem is a **dramatic monologue**. This means it is a poem where the speaker reveals things about himself to the reader.
    a   What facts do we learn about the Duchess in the poem?
    b   What do other people think about the Duchess?
    c   Look at what the Duke thinks of her. What does he disapprove of in her words and actions?
    d   What do these things reveal about her, and about him?

3   Look at lines 33–43. What do you find out about the Duke's view of himself in these lines?

4   In line 46, what is the effect of the line break after the phrase 'There she stands'? Think about what comes next.

5   The Duke stops looking at the portrait after 'As if alive' (line 47). What do you learn about the Duke after this point in the poem?

Words/phrases to explore (A01)

ACTIVITY 2

1   The last two words of the poem are 'for me'. Why do you think the writer chose these as the last words?

2   How do they form a suitable end for the whole poem? You could write a paragraph about the Duke starting from those words.

GradeStudio

Sample answer

To achieve a C on this AO1 descriptor, you need to show **sustained response to elements of text**. The following extract from a sample answer would hit the grade C requirement.

> The Duke appears to admire other people, like Frà Pandolf, but really he only admires himself. He is the only person allowed to draw back the curtain over the picture, and he chooses 'never to stoop' as that would lessen his importance in his own eyes. He demands that others admire him too, and when the Duchess dares to 'approve' of anybody else, the Duke thinks they are 'fools' and disapproves of her so much it seems that he had her killed.

The River God

by Stevie Smith

Read the poem in your AQA Anthology, then complete the activities below.

ACTIVITY 1

Initial responses

1   What sort of character does the god seem to be to you?
    Think about:
    • what he enjoys
    • his attitude to the woman
    • what he thinks of himself
    • the words he uses to show what he thinks.

2   How does the writer make the voice seem like a god? Look at the attitudes the voice has, and the words it uses. 'Where my fish float by' suggests he owns them, for example. What else can you find?

3   The river god is a spirit of water. Find as many references to water and rivers as you can, starting with the second line.

4   Look at lines 17–18. What is the god's attitude to the things in his river here? Look carefully at both lines.

5   Look at the **rhyme** in the poem.
    a   How does the **rhyme scheme** change in the last four lines?
    b   Why do you think the writer chooses to rhyme 'bed' and 'head'?
    c   'Head' and 'her' do not rhyme. Why do you think the writer chose not to rhyme the last two lines?
    d   What effect does the last line have? Notice that it's a sentence all in one line.

6   Look at the repetitions and **exclamations** in the poem, like 'Hi yih, yippity-yap'. What effects do they have on your impression of the god?

▶ Poem Glossary

weir a low dam built across a river, which causes water to flow quickly downstream

GradeStudio

Sample answer Ⓑ

To achieve a B on this AO1 descriptor, you need to make a **considered response**. To do this, you need to think about more than one thing. The following extract from a sample answer would hit the grade B requirement:

> **Activity 1, question 1**
> In some ways the god seems to be kind, as he blesses the fish and seems to like people swimming, and having fun. It is very sinister fun, though, as it includes a deliberate drowning and imprisonment of the body.

ACTIVITY 2

Words/phrases to explore (AO1 and AO2)

What overall effect does the voice of the god have on you, the reader? Do you like him, or not?

The Hunchback in the Park

by Dylan Thomas

Read the poem in your AQA Anthology,
then complete the activities below.

Initial responses

ACTIVITY 1

1 What are your first impressions of the hunchback?
   Find details from the poem to support what you think.

2 In the first **stanza**, the hunchback enters when the lock is
   opened, like the trees and water. This makes him seem more
   like part of nature than human. Now look carefully through
   the rest of the poem and write down examples of words and
   phrases that make him seem part of nature.

3 The writer also shows him as being like an animal. Starting
   with line 11, find examples of where the writer does this.

4 In the fourth stanza, the trees are described as a 'loud zoo'. Why?
   Think of as many reasons as you can. Try seeing the phrase from all
   the points of view in the poem – the boys, the hunchback, and the
   speaker in the poem.

5 In the fifth stanza, how does the writer get inside the minds of the
   boys? Think about what they are imagining.

6 In the sixth stanza, how does the writer get inside the mind of the
   hunchback? What does this stanza show about what he thinks?

7 a In the last stanza, what things have followed the hunchback out
      of the park? How?
   b Now think about the word 'unmade'. How has the park been
      'unmade'?

Words/phrases to explore (AO1)

ACTIVITY 2

Think again about the 'I' in the second stanza. Using details from the
poem:

1 Who do you think he is, and how old is he?

2 What do you think his response is to the hunchback, and to the
   boys?

GradeStudio

Sample answer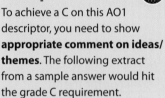

To achieve a C on this AO1
descriptor, you need to show
**appropriate comment on ideas/
themes**. The following extract
from a sample answer would hit
the grade C requirement.

Activity 1, question 6

It would be easy to see
the hunchback as some
sort of old pervert
because he imagines a
woman, but the key thing
is that he imagines her
'straight', 'straight and
tall', unlike his 'crooked
bones'. He imagines
what he would like to
be, just like the boys
who imagine 'tigers' and
'sailors' in the woods.

The Ruined Maid

by Thomas Hardy

Read the poem in your AQA Anthology, then complete the activities below.

▶ **Poem Glossary**

spudding up docks digging up weeds

barton barn

megrims migraine

Initial responses

ACTIVITY 1

1 **a** Who are the two **speakers** in the poem?
   b What are the differences between the speakers?

2 What does the first speaker admire about the second? If you look for all the individual things you might come to a general view.

3 **a** In the fourth **stanza** the first speaker says about Melia 'your little gloves fit as on any la-dy!' Why might she be surprised by this?
   b What do you think she means by 'la-dy' here? For example, is she being ironic?

4 How is the speech of the two characters different, and what does it show about them?

5 The **rhyme scheme** is very simple. Why do you think Hardy has chosen to do this?

6 In each stanza except the last, the first speaker has the third line and Melia the fourth. How does the **rhyme** make the lines seem more like conversation?

7 The last stanza is different, as Melia has the last two lines to herself. Why do you think Hardy has chosen to do this at the end?

GradeStudio

Sample answer ◉

To achieve a C on this AO2 descriptor, you need to show **appropriate comment on ideas/themes**. To do this, you need to think of more than one idea about the poem. The following extract from a sample answer would hit the grade B requirement.

> Activity 1, question 2
> Melia is admired by her country friend as she has escaped a miserable existence by being 'ruined'. There is some irony here because Melia is not really a lady at all.

Words/phrases to explore (AO1 and AO2)

ACTIVITY 2

'You ain't ruined' says Melia at the end of the poem.

1 How far is each of the characters 'ruined'?

2 Think about the title. Which of the two women does this apply to most?

Casehistory: Alison (head injury)

by U. A. Fanthorpe

Read the poem in your AQA Anthology, then complete the activities below.

Initial responses

1   What exactly is wrong with Alison?

2   The poem opens with (*She looks at her photograph*). What effect do you think this has on the reader? Imagine how Alison feels.

3   The first **stanza** reads a bit like a puzzle.
    a   When the reader has worked it out, why does Alison not know her younger self?
    b   Reading it again, what is the effect of the last word of the first stanza? Think about the tense used.

4   Why do you think the writer chooses to single out the word 'Hardly' as she does, after a break between stanzas and before a full stop? What can Alison's knee 'hardly' do?

5   In stanzas 5 and 6, what did the younger Alison do which the older woman can't?

6   Why do you think the writer uses the word 'her' three times in stanza 8? Think about the effect of this repetition.

7   Why do you think the writer places 'A bright girl she was' on a separate line at the end of the poem? What is the effect of this line?

Words/phrases to explore (AO1 and AO2)

Alison seems to feel sorry for her younger self.

1   Why do you think she feels this way?

2   Do you sympathise with Alison? Why? You could write a paragraph explaining your response. Remember to support what you think from the poem.

▶ **Poem Glossary**

autocratic regal, queenly

Degas dancer Degas was a French impressionist artist. Many of his portraits were of ballet dancers

GradeStudio

Sample answer D

To achieve a D on this AO2 descriptor, you need to show **identification of effect(s) of writers' choices of language and/or structure and/or form intended/achieved**. To do this, you need to suggest what a device is being used for. The following extract from a sample answer would hit the grade D requirement because it identifies the effect of the structure of the final line.

> Activity 1, question 7
> The writer puts 'a bright girl she was' on a line on its own at the end to show the reader how sad the speaker is about her life.

To move to the C band, the answer would have to **explain** exactly how this works.

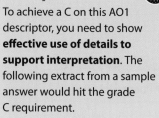

GradeStudio

Sample answer ⓒ

To achieve a C on this AO1 descriptor, you need to show **effective use of details to support interpretation**. The following extract from a sample answer would hit the grade C requirement.

> **Activity 1, question 7**
>
> The speaker is determined to show the realities of what happens to the body after death, to show that there is no life after death. His eyes are full of 'maggots', his 'finger-bones/Stick through his finger-ends', and his mouth is full of earth. All this leads to the word at the end of the poem, 'decay'.

On a Portrait of a Deaf Man

by John Betjeman

Read the poem in your AQA Anthology, then complete the activities below.

Initial responses
ACTIVITY 1

1 What does the **speaker** of the poem feel about his father overall? Find evidence to support what you think. You could start with the first adjective in the poem.

2 List all of the activities which the 'deaf man' used to like. How do these work to create the character of the 'deaf man'?

3 How does the writer play with the idea of eating in a gruesome way in the second **stanza**?

4 The fourth stanza is also deliberately gruesome. How does the writer use **rhyme** to add to the effect? Look at what he connects together with rhyme.

5 Now look at the seventh stanza. Like stanzas 2 and 4, there is a gruesome idea here about the corpse.
   a How are these stanzas structured in a similar way?
   b How does the writer use rhyme to add to the effect?

6 There is another rhyme in the last stanza which works in a similar way. What two things does the rhyme connect? How do they contrast with each other as well?

7 The poem finishes with the line 'I only see decay.' How does the whole poem and the **imagery** in it lead up to this last word?

Words/phrases to explore (AO1)
ACTIVITY 2

John Betjeman was in many ways a religious man. What do you think the last sentence of the poem says about his belief?

Looking at the poems individually: what have you learned?

My learning ▶

In this section you will:
- think about which poems interested you most and why.

Complete Activities 1 and 2 below. As you do, think about which poems and which features of poems were most interesting to you.

Note that the words in bold in the tasks below refer to the key words in the Assessment Objectives.

Assessment Objective 1 (AO1)

ACTIVITY 1

1 Which of these poems did you **respond** to most strongly? You may have liked it, or disliked it, or found it the most interesting, or horrible. You may have a number of things to say about it.

2 Which poems did you find it easiest to offer an **interpretation** about? In other words, you had an opinion about a poem's meaning and could argue from the text and **select detail** to support your opinion. For instance, you might have found it easy to argue that the shopkeeper in 'Singh Song' neglects his shop because he is ordered about by his bride.

 Suggesting more than one interpretation of a poem, or parts of a poem, gives you opportunities to score more marks. For instance, there are several ways in which you could respond to the shopkeeper.

Assessment Objective 2 (AO2)

ACTIVITY 2

1 Which features of **language**, **structure** or **form** did you understand best? The most promising ones to write about in the exam will be the ones where you have most to say. For instance, you might have found several things to say about:
- the effect of the repetitions in 'Checking Out Me History' (language)
- the repetition of 'a bright girl she was' at the end of 'Case history: Alison' (structure)
- the effects of the rhyme at the end of 'The Clown Punk' (form).

 When answering this question, it would be best if you chose your own examples rather than using the ones above!

2 What **ideas** did you pick out in the poems? Again, the best answers will probably identify more than one idea in a poem, or several aspects of one idea. For instance, you might have identified attitudes to women in 'Les Grands Seigneurs' or 'My Last Duchess'. Which poems contain ideas about history?

My learning ▶

In this section you will learn how to:
- compare poems and address the Assessment Objectives
- develop writing skills and practise exam-style questions.

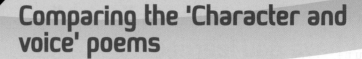

Comparing the 'Character and voice' poems

Assessment Objective 3 is broken into two parts:

▶ comparing ideas and themes in the poems, with detail

▶ comparing the ways writers use language or structure or form, with detail.

In responding to the exam question, you will need to address both these parts.

Assessment Objective:

The Assessment Objective you will be focusing on in this part of the chapter is:

 make comparisons and explain links between texts, evaluating writers' different ways of expressing meaning and achieving effects.

Comparing ideas and themes

Read the poems 'The Clown Punk' and 'The Hunchback in the Park', then complete the activities below.

ACTIVITY 1

Think about the ideas and themes in the two poems. List as many similarities and differences as you can. Think about:
- what both the main characters in the poems have in common
- how other people respond to the two characters
- how the two main characters differ.

ACTIVITY 2

Using your list of similarities and differences from Activity 1, decide how different each of the poems are for each point you made. For example, the young people in both poems react badly to the main character – but exactly how do they react, and how do you think these reactions are different?

Your answer needs to be based on the detail in the poems, so you need to quote or refer to specific parts of the poem to support what you think.

GradeStudio

Sample answer

To hit one of the AO3 descriptors at grade E, you need to make **some comment(s) on similarities/ differences, with detail**.

The following extract from a sample answer would hit the grade E requirement.

> The two characters are compared to things that belong to the places where they are. The clown punk is compared to a basket of washing, which seems more like a town thing, but the hunchback is compared to the birds and the water in the park that he goes to every day.

Now you need to compare the differences in the ways the poems are written.

- What comparisons did you find in the poems? What sort of things do they describe? Are the comparisons similar in what they describe, or in the effects they have when you read them?
- Which of the poems use **rhyme**? Why do you think the writers of the poems use rhyme, or not?
- Compare the endings of the two poems. How does each ending finish the poem off, both in what it says and the ways it is said? Are there any similarities between the two endings, do you think?

GradeStudio

Sample answer

To hit one of the AO3 descriptors at grade D, you need to make some **structured comments on similarities/differences, with detail**. The following extract from a sample answer would hit the grade D requirement.

The two characters are both compared to things that belong to the places where they are. The clown punk is compared to a basket of washing, which seems more like a town thing, but the hunchback is compared to the birds and the water in the park that he goes to every day. The ways the lines are written make the hunchback seem more organised, though: 'Like the park birds' then 'like the water' on the next line sounds like two organised movements, not happening very quickly. The lines about the clown punk don't seem as organised, and the 'basket of washing' isn't an organised idea at all.

Comparing writers' methods

One of the best ways to score well when comparing poems is to compare two details, one from each poem, that you can say a lot about when you put them together. It doesn't matter whether you're comparing what the details are about, or the ways they're written, though if you're dealing with both it will provide more to say.

For instance, let's suppose that you chose these two details from these poems:

> like a basket of washing that got up and walked

(The Clown Punk)

> Like the park birds he came early
> Like the water he sat down

(The Hunchback in the Park)

You could say that these are both **similes**, but that would only be a simple link between the details, which is in the F band of marks. What more can you find to say? Think about:

- the places where the two characters are, and how the comparisons fit the places
- what the comparisons say about the characters – what they look like or what they are like as people
- how the lines, and the way they are arranged, suit walking (Clown Punk) or sitting (Hunchback).

You should have enough material now to write a good paragraph comparing the two details. Try it.

Putting it all together

To practise the skills you've been working on in these activities, here are some more activities on a different pair of poems: 'On a Portrait of a Deaf Man' and 'Casehistory: Alison.'

ACTIVITY 5

1 What ideas and themes can you find in the poems which are similar? For example, both the main characters in the poems are damaged in some way. How are they each damaged? Is the damage similar in any way, or different? Which damage is worse, do you think?

2 There are three types of damage in 'Portrait of a Deaf Man' – two to the father, and one to the **speaker** of the poem, the son. How are each of these types of damage different, or similar, to the damage in 'Casehistory'?

3 What attitude does each speaker have to the damaged person? Are the attitudes similar in any way? How?

4 Now you need to think about how the poems are written. You could say that one poem rhymes and the other doesn't, but that is only a simple link, which belongs in grade F, so you need to think a bit more.

   • How does Betjeman use **rhyme** to emphasise the gruesome ideas about the decay of his father's body in 'Portrait of a Deaf Man'? Think which words are connected by the rhymes at the ends of some of the **stanzas**.

   • Fanthorpe does not use rhyme to convey the damage to the character, but she does use **form** – how the lines are set out. How does she make the lines deliberately jagged, to suit the damage that Alison has suffered? How is the effect very different to the Betjeman poem?

Comparing writers' methods and purposes   ACTIVITY 6

Now choose two details, one from each poem, that you think you could compare. Let's suppose you chose the endings of each poem – the last line of 'Casehistory' and the last stanza of 'Portrait of a Deaf Man'.

• Why do you think Betjeman rhymes 'pray' with 'decay' at the end of 'Portrait of a Deaf Man'? Think what he is saying about his religious faith here.

• Why do you think Fanthorpe places the last line of 'Casehistory: Alison' on a line by itself?

• How is the last word of each poem an important word in the poem as a whole?

Now you could write a paragraph, or more, comparing the effects of the endings of the two poems. Try it.

GradeStudio

Sample answer

To hit one of the AO3 descriptors at grade C, you need to show **sustained focus on similarities/differences** with material for a range of comparisons. The following extract from a sample answer to Activity 6 would hit the grade C requirement.

There is a lot of damage to the characters in both poems. The father in 'Portrait of a Deaf Man' was deaf in his life, so that he knew 'ev'ry bird/But not the song it sung'. In death, though, his body is decaying in a gruesome way. There are 'maggots in his eyes' and 'his finger-bones/Stick through his finger-ends'. Alison is still alive, but her body has changed for the worse too. She is 'Enmeshed in comforting fat' instead of 'delicate' and her knees 'hardly' lug her up the stairs. The mental change is worse, though. She can't remember her father's death from one day to the next, whereas she used to be 'bright' and passed A Levels. There is no sense of any change like that in the father before he died. 'He would have liked to say goodbye' suggests that he died suddenly, but unchanged, unlike Alison.

GradeStudio

Sample answer B

To hit one of the AO3 descriptors at grade B, you need to show **developed comparison** with thoughtful selection of material for comparison. The following extract from a sample answer would hit the grade B requirement, especially if it followed on from the paragraph above. The writing would have moved on from a sustained focus on one aspect of the poems, i.e. the damage to the characters, to another, developing the comparison.

The characters in both poems have a happy past, and seem to be admired. The father in 'Deaf Man' was 'kind' and 'wise' and seems to have enjoyed life, such as 'potatoes in their skins' and 'Cornish air'; similarly, 'smiles' are mentioned three times in describing the younger Alison, and she is admired for her 'delicate angles', 'poise', her achievements, and being 'bright'. There are already shadows in the father, though: he is deaf, and seems to have a dread of death in his reaction to Highgate cemetery. There are no such shadows about Alison: even when she grieves for her father, she smiles.

My learning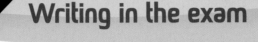

In this section you will learn how to:
● structure a response in the exam
● use the skills you have learned to perform successfully.

Assessment Objectives:

 A01 respond to texts critically and imaginatively; select and evaluate relevant textual detail to illustrate and support interpretations.

 A02 explain how language, structure and form contribute to writers' presentation of ideas, themes and settings.

 A03 make comparisons and explain links between texts, evaluating writers' different ways of expressing meaning and achieving effects.

Writing in the exam

Writing your response – planning and structuring

Your process with any exam question should be:

Read

Read the questions – what exactly are you being asked to do? The questions should remind you about the Assessment Objectives. There will be a choice of two questions, so you need to make a choice quickly. Each question will ask you to compare a named poem with an unnamed poem, so your choice might be based on the poem that is named, or on what each question is asking you to do.

Think

This is the planning stage. The first word of the exam task is likely to be 'compare'. One of the descriptors in the mark band for a grade C is 'sustained focus on similarities/differences'. This suggests that a wise course of action would be to build your response around a comparison of the two poems.

This doesn't mean that everything you write should be comparative. You should decide how you're going to compare the poems before you write. Use a plan like the one on page 28. Within that, you need to jot down some of the ideas from the poems and perhaps one or two details that you're planning to use – you should choose things that you can write quite a lot about.

The thinking is more important than the writing here. The whole process might take 5 minutes, perhaps (certainly not less than 2 minutes). You only have 45 minutes for the whole task. Don't start writing straight away, think about the question carefully first!

Write

When you write, what you are going to show is:

▶ what you think about the poems

▶ why they are written in the ways that they are

▶ what happens when you compare the poems, or parts of them.

In other words, these are the things the Assessment Objectives focus on. The phrase 'or parts of them', is important. No question will ask you to write down everything you know about the poems; you have to select from what you know to think and write about the poems in answer to this question, in the ways that you've practised as you've worked through this section.

Edit

If you have any time left, you should look for ways to improve your answer. Don't look for spelling or punctuation errors: these don't carry marks here. Could you quickly add another possible meaning of a word or phrase that you've written about? Is there another idea about the effect of a writer's choice of language? Additions of this kind might gain you an extra mark.

Putting it into practice

Let's take a typical exam question:

'Compare (AO3) the ways the writers present (AO2) the voices of the central character in 'Singh Song' and one other poem from 'Character and voice' (AO1).

Let's suppose that you chose 'The River God' as a good choice to compare with 'Singh Song' – they are both cheerful male voices and they are both about a relationship with a woman, partly at least, but they are very different personalities and presented very differently. First, jot down a few ideas from the poems that you're going to use when you write. You could use the method shown below.

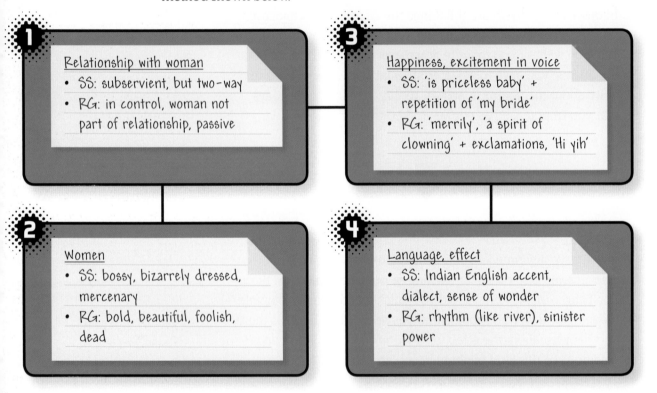

1

Relationship with woman
- SS: subservient, but two-way
- RG: in control, woman not part of relationship, passive

2

Women
- SS: bossy, bizarrely dressed, mercenary
- RG: bold, beautiful, foolish, dead

3

Happiness, excitement in voice
- SS: 'is priceless baby' + repetition of 'my bride'
- RG: 'merrily', 'a spirit of clowning' + exclamations, 'Hi yih'

4

Language, effect
- SS: Indian English accent, dialect, sense of wonder
- RG: rhythm (like river), sinister power

In the notes above, the student has identified two ideas about the characters in the poems, and two ideas about the ways in which voice is created. Some details to use have been jotted down. There are a lot more ideas that you could think of, but the task is not to try to offer an exhaustive account – you are just showing off the skills of thinking and writing that you have, so four is plenty.

After thinking of the four ideas, the student decided on the order they should go in (indicated by the numbers).

Read the extracts from these sample student answers, together with the question below and the examiner comments. You could then try the sample exam question on page 31.

Compare the ways the writers present the voices of the central character in 'Singh Song' and one other poem from 'Character and voice'.

Openings

 D grade answer

Student A

The speaker in 'Singh Song' obviously loves his 'bride'. He says they 'made luv like vee rowing through Putney'. He loves her more than he should, because he locks the door even when the shop should be open, so that the shoppers cry, 'Hey Singh, ver yoo bin?' The writer shows how much he loves her by the way he uses their conversation at the end about the moon, and how much it costs.

Examiner comment

Student A's response is scoring some marks already, because there is a **supported response** (E) about Singh's love, and then an **explained response** (D) about why he loves her 'more than he should'. The response **identifies the effect** (D) of the conversation at the end but doesn't **explain** it (C). There is no comparison yet, either.

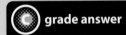 **C grade answer**

Student B

There are very different relationships between the speakers and women in the two poems I have chosen. In 'The River God' the god is entirely in control of the woman, and gets nothing back from her, except 'the fear she looks at me with'. Singh's bride seems to be in control of him, tempting him away from his job, but he certainly gets something back from her, as they make love 'like vee rowing through Putney'. They both seem to love the women, though. The god refers to the woman as his 'beautiful dear' and admires her 'golden sleepy head'. Singh loves sitting with his bride, and the writer shows his love by mentioning the moon, which conjures up romance, and by ending their conversation with 'Is priceless baby', so that the final word of the poem shows his love.

Examiner comment

Student B's response uses comparison from the beginning, and has already achieved **structured comments on similarities/ differences** (D), with **details for a range of comparisons** (D). This time there's an **effect explained** (C) about the end of 'Singh Song', one band better than student A.

Examiner comment

Both openings above get straight on with the task, though. They avoid using 'In this essay I am going to write about...', which is a waste of time.

A paragraph on Assessment Objective 1

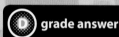

E grade answer

Student A

The women in the two poems are very different. The woman in 'River God' is good looking, because she's described as having a 'beautiful white face' and a 'golden sleepy head'. The bride in 'Singh Song' seems to look very odd, though, with her 'tiny eyes' and 'tummy like a teddy', and the peculiar clothes she wears.

Examiner comment

Student A's paragraph has two **supported responses** (E), and **some comment on similarity** (E), **supported** (E).

D grade answer

Student B

The women in the two poems are very different. The woman in 'The River God' is good looking, because she's described as having a 'beautiful white face' and a 'golden sleepy head'. The bride in 'Singh Song' seems to look very odd, though, with her 'tiny eyes' and 'tummy like a teddy'. Her clothes don't seem to make her attractive, either, because the colours clash, and wearing a sari with a donkey jacket seems very inelegant. They are different in character, too. The woman in 'The River God' was 'bold', because she bathed in the wrong place in the river, but now she's passive, because she's dead, whereas the bride is very much alive, and not passive at all. She makes love, is busy on the computer, curses Singh's family and watches for thieves.

Examiner comment

Student B's paragraph starts in the same way, but there is an **explained response** (D) to what the bride looks like, and **structured comment on similarity/difference** (D), because the student adds another comparison about the women.

A paragraph on Assessment Objective 2 A02

Student A

The writers of the poems use different methods to show the two voices. The voice in 'Singh Song' repeats 'my bride' to show you how he feels, and in 'The River God' there are lots of exclamations, like 'Hi yih, yippity-yap'.

Examiner comment

Student A has some **awareness of a writer's use of language** (E) twice, but in neither case does the student suggest what effect they might have. 'To show you how he feels' isn't saying anything exact. There isn't a comment on comparison – the two things seem to be just different because they're different, rather than being linked.

Student B

The writers of the poems use different methods to show the emotions of the two voices. Singh's happiness is shown by the repetitions of 'my bride' at the beginning of three consecutive stanzas, and 'The River God' has exclamations which show his happiness and excitement. 'Hi yih, yippity-yap' sounds happy because of the joyful nonsense words, but also the rhythm is like a quickly flowing river, as though the words are tumbling over each other.

Examiner comment

Student B **identifies the effect** (D) of the repetitions of 'my bride', and then **explains the effect** (C) of 'Hi yih'. There is a **comment on comparison** (E) here, too, as the student states that they both show happiness.

You are now ready to tackle an exam question. Here's one to try:

Compare how characters in difficulties are presented in 'Give' and one other poem from 'Character and voice'.

When you've written your answer you could mark it, or get a partner to mark it, using the mark scheme on page 142.

Further comparison activities

Below are some comparison activities that you could attempt for each of the poems in the 'Character and voice' cluster.

The Clown Punk

1 **Comparing ideas and themes**
Compare the attitudes to a disadvantaged person in 'The Clown Punk' and 'The Hunchback in the Park'.
2 **Comparing writers' devices**
Compare the ways in which the writers present a disadvantaged person in 'The Clown Punk' and 'The Hunchback in the Park'.

Checking Out Me History

1 **Comparing ideas and themes**
Compare the attitudes that the speakers have to history in 'Checking Out Me History' and 'Horse Whisperer'.
2 **Comparing writers' devices**
Compare the ways that the writers use repetitions in 'Checking Out Me History' and 'Brendon Gallacher'. What effects do the repetitions have?

Horse Whisperer

1 **Comparing ideas and themes**
Compare the situations of the central characters in 'Horse Whisperer' and 'The Hunchback in the Park'.
2 **Comparing writers' devices**
Compare the ways in which the writers establish character in 'Horse Whisperer' and 'My Last Duchess'.

Medusa

1 **Comparing ideas and themes**
Compare the attitudes to men in 'Medusa' and 'Les Grands Seigneurs'.
2 **Comparing writers' devices**
Compare the effects of the ways the endings are written in 'Medusa' and 'Les Grands Seigneurs'.

Singh Song

1 **Comparing ideas and themes**
Compare the attitudes to women in 'Singh Song' and 'My Last Duchess'.
2 **Comparing writers' devices**
Compare the ways in which the **speaker's** voice is created in 'Singh Song' and 'The River God'.

Brendon Gallacher

1 **Comparing ideas and themes**
Compare the central characters in 'Brendon Gallacher' and 'On a Portrait of a Deaf Man'.
2 **Comparing writers' devices**
Compare the ways in which the writers create sympathy for the **speakers** in 'Brendon Gallacher' and 'On a Portrait of a Deaf Man'.

Give

1 **Comparing ideas and themes**
Compare the attitudes of the voices in 'Give' and 'Medusa' to the person they are speaking to.
2 **Comparing writers' devices**
Compare the writing of the last two lines of 'Give' with the last two lines of 'The Clown Punk'. Look at the length of the sentences, the effects of the full stops and the rhymes, and the effects of the last four words of each poem.

Les Grands Seigneurs

1 **Comparing ideas and themes**
Compare the attitudes to men in 'Les Grands Seigneurs' and 'Medusa'.

2 **Comparing writers' devices**
Compare the ways in which voice is created in 'Les Grands Seigneurs' and 'My Last Duchess'.

Ozymandias

1 **Comparing ideas and themes**
Compare the central characters in 'Ozymandias' and 'My Last Duchess'.

2 **Comparing writers' devices**
Compare the ways that character is created in 'Ozymandias' and 'My Last Duchess'.

My Last Duchess

1 **Comparing ideas and themes**
Compare the characters and situations of the duchess in 'My Last Duchess' and the central character in 'Les Grands Seigneurs'.

2 **Comparing writers' devices**
Compare the ways in which the voice of the speaker is created in 'My Last Duchess' and 'The River God'.

The River God

1 **Comparing ideas and themes**
Compare the central characters in 'The River God' and 'Medusa'.

2 **Comparing writers' devices**
Compare the ways the characters in 'The River God' and 'Medusa' are shown to have power.

The Hunchback in the Park

1 **Comparing ideas and themes**
Compare the central characters of 'The Hunchback in the Park' and 'The Clown Punk'.

2 **Comparing writers' devices**
Compare the ways the central characters are created in 'The Hunchback in the Park' and 'The Clown Punk'.

The Ruined Maid

1 **Comparing ideas and themes**
Compare the ways in which women are presented in 'The Ruined Maid' and 'Les Grands Seigneurs'.

2 **Comparing writers' devices**
Compare the ways in which conversation and **dialect** are shown in 'The Ruined Maid' and 'Singh Song'.

Casehistory: Alison

1 **Comparing ideas and themes**
Compare the central characters in 'Casehistory: Alison' and 'Medusa'.

2 **Comparing writers' devices**
Compare the effects of the endings of 'Casehistory: Alison' and 'Medusa'.

On a Portrait of a Deaf Man

1 **Comparing ideas and themes**
Compare the feelings of the speakers in 'On a Portrait of a Deaf Man' and 'Brendon Gallacher'.

2 **Comparing writers' devices**
Compare the effects of the endings of 'On a Portrait of a Deaf Man' and 'Ozymandias'.

In this section you will learn how to:
● become familiar with the poems as a whole
● start to make links between the poems.

Getting to know the poems

Assessment Objectives:

 A01 respond to texts critically and imaginatively; select and evaluate relevant textual detail to illustrate and support interpretations.

 A02 explain how language, structure and form contribute to writers' presentation of ideas, themes and settings.

 A03 make comparisons and explain links between texts, evaluating writers' different ways of expressing meaning and achieving effects.

The poems

The Blackbird of Glanmore
Seamus Heaney

A Vision
Simon Armitage

The Moment
Margaret Atwood

Cold Knap Lake
Gillian Clarke

Price We Pay for the Sun
Grace Nichols

Neighbours
Gillian Clarke

Crossing the Loch
Kathleen Jamie

Hard Water
Jean Sprackland

London
William Blake

The Prelude (extract)
William Wordsworth

The Wild Swans at Coole
W. B. Yeats

Spellbound
Emily Brontë

Below the Green Corrie
Norman McCaig

Storm in the Black Forest
D. H. Lawrence

Wind
Ted Hughes

Introduction

The poems in this chapter focus on place, and the relationship between places and people. All the poems are in your AQA Anthology.

In this chapter you will be:

▶ looking at the individual poems

▶ comparing the poems

▶ learning how to approach exam questions.

This preparation will help you develop your writing skills in order to hit the Assessment Objectives. See page v for more information about what the Assessment Objectives mean. In the exam you will have to compare two poems from this chapter.

Getting started

The first thing to do is to start to get to know the 'Place' poems.

ACTIVITY 1

Read all the 'Place' poems in your AQA Anthology. Just notice what they seem to be about – don't worry about trying to make sense of every line.

ACTIVITY 2

Write the headings listed below on a sheet of paper. Under each heading make notes of any links between poems. Include poems that have similarities and differences. Use the tips below to help you.

Headings	Tips
What the poems are about	All the poems are about places, but there are very different attitudes to place. Which poems seem to have similar attitudes? Which have similar **tones**? Think about whether the poems seem reflective, happy, melancholy, or something else.
Beginnings/endings	Find examples of poems which end with a definite statement. Which endings seem to summarise the message or the mood of the poems?
Length	You might notice some distinct similarities or differences. Include the number and length of **stanzas**, if there are any.
Rhyme	Is there a regular **rhyme scheme**? Does it change? Be careful – some poems that don't seem to rhyme often use a lot of **half-rhyme** or **echoes**, like 'Cold Knap Lake', which has one **rhyming couplet** at the end. If you were working on this poem, you'd need to consider why the writer does this. 'London' rhymes all the way through, though – how does this add to the feeling Blake is creating?
Rhythm	Are there any poems with a strong **rhythm**, such as 'The Wild Swans at Coole'? Are any of the others similar to this?
Language	Some poems have striking **imagery**, such as 'Below the Green Corrie' and 'The Moment'. See if there are any similarities. Both 'Cold Knap Lake' and 'The Wild Swans at Coole' make use of swans, but differently – how? There's a lot of **personification**, too – look for it.

Now display your findings on a sheet of A3 paper in one of the following ways.

1   Spread the titles out on the sheet and draw links between them, labelling each one.

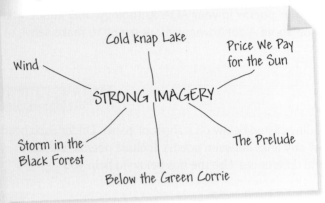

2   Draw a picture or symbol for each idea (such as death or nature) that appears in more than one poem, and group the poems around each – a poem can appear in more than one group.

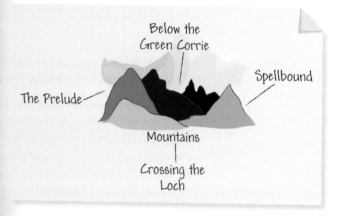

3   Draw a picture, or pictures, for each poem on the sheet, and link similar ones with arrows.

In these activities you have started to tackle all three Assessment Objectives. Now you will be focusing on AO1 and AO2 as you look at the poems individually (pages 37–53). You will return to AO3 when you compare the poems (pages 54–57). Finally, you will look at how to turn your knowledge and skills into successful exam answers, before you attempt one yourself (pages 58–65).

Looking at the poems individually

My learning ▶

In this section you will learn how to:
- develop your responses to the poems
- relate the Assessment Objectives to the poems.

This section of the chapter, pages 37–53, will lead you through each individual poem. Throughout, you will find examples of student responses at different levels.

In the exam you will have to write about the poems individually. You will also have to compare two poems; one named poem and one unnamed poem, which means you can choose the second one.

Assessment Objectives:

The Assessment Objectives you will be focusing on in this part of the chapter are:

 respond to texts critically and imaginatively; select and evaluate relevant textual detail to illustrate and support interpretations.

 explain how language, structure and form contribute to writers' presentation of ideas, themes and settings.

The Blackbird of Glanmore
by Seamus Heaney

Read the poem in your AQA Anthology, then complete the activities below.

Initial responses

ACTIVITY 1

1 a Read through the whole poem. Where is the **speaker** visiting, and what does he see while he is there?
   b Which other people have lived there in the past?

2 In the poem, the speaker thinks about his life. Look at the two lines beginning 'I park'. How does Heaney suggest a sense of reflection here by the words, the punctuation and the shape of the lines?

3 Look at the three lines beginning 'And I think of one gone to him'.
   a Who has the brother gone to?
   b How was he like the blackbird?
   c Why do you think Heaney describes the brother as 'Haunter-son'? Who and where did he haunt?

4 What did the neighbour think about the bird? Look at the words he uses.

5 a 'The automatic lock/Clunks shut'. How do these words break the silence and reflection?
   b How does Heaney use the sound of words here to make the moment sharper?

6 In the three lines beginning 'I've a bird's eye view', Heaney imagines how the blackbird sees him, but there is more to it than just a point of view.
   a How could he be 'a shadow' in his 'house of life'?
   b What does this make the blackbird seem to be, looking down on him?

7 The last line, 'In the ivy when I leave', is repeated from earlier in the poem, but this time as a line on its own. Why do you think the writer does this? What is the effect?

Words/phrases to explore (AO1 and AO2)

ACTIVITY 2

'In the ivy when I leave'. How is the blackbird made to seem as though it's always there in the whole poem?

A Vision

by Simon Armitage

Read the poem in your AQA Anthology, then complete the activities below.

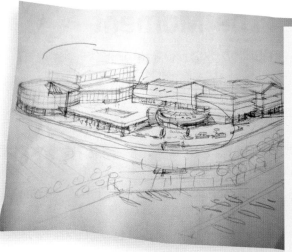

▶ **Poem Glossary**

balsa wood a light wood often used for making models

cantilevered supported by beams

Fuzzy-Felt a child's toy consisting of a flocked backing board and a number of felt shapes that can be used to create many different pictures

Fuzzy-Felt grass a piece of green material to look like grass on the model

boulevard a broad avenue, usually lined by trees

Initial responses

ACTIVITY 1

1 What is the future town like? Find supporting details for what you think.

2 a What does the **speaker** in the poem think about the future town?
   b How is that attitude shown in the first **stanza**?

3 Look at the second stanza. What makes the 'vision' seem unreal?

4 a What is there in the second stanza that suggests someone is playing? You should be able to find three things.
   b Can you find a similar idea in the third stanza?

5 a Which word in the fourth stanza suggests that the town is very 'grand' for ordinary people?
   b Which other words in the poem suggest the same thing?

6 How does Armitage show in the last stanza that the 'vision' was unreal, and never happened? Think about:
   a the words he uses here which are different from the words in the rest of the poem
   b what you associate with a 'landfill site'
   c his choice for the last word.

Words/phrases to explore (AO1 and AO2)

ACTIVITY 2

Look at the first line again. How exactly does this line set up the whole poem? Think about what it says and the choices Armitage has made of words and punctuation.

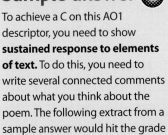

GradeStudio

Sample answer **C**

To achieve a C on this AO1 descriptor, you need to show **sustained response to elements of text.** To do this, you need to write several connected comments about what you think about the poem. The following extract from a sample answer would hit the grade C requirement:

> Activity 2
> The future place was supposed to be 'beautiful', and even magical for the people living in it. 'Smoked glass' and 'tubular steel' suggest a very modern place, like the 'electric cars'. 'Fairground rides' and 'like dreams' suggest the magic of the place, and 'strolling the boulevard' suggests a lazy, easy life. It wasn't real, though – it didn't happen.

The Moment

by Margaret Atwood

Read the poem in your AQA Anthology, then complete the activities below.

GradeStudio

Sample answer ▢

To achieve an E on this AO2 descriptor, you need to show **awareness of writers' choice(s) of language and/ or structure and/or form**. The following extract from a sample answer would hit the grade E requirement.

> **Activity 1, question 4**
> The writer makes the reader pause after 'I own this' to emphasise something.

To move to the D band you would have to say what the 'something' is – that is, to say what the writer intended to do. To move to the C band you would have to explain how it does this.

Initial responses

ACTIVITY 1

1 In the whole poem, why does man think he owns nature? How doesn't he own it?

2 'A long voyage' could mean a sea voyage. Do you think that a sea voyage is being described, or another sort of voyage?

3 In lines 3 and 4, there is a list of places. Think where each one is, and decide how the list works. What direction does it move in?

4 Why do you think the writer places a gap between **stanzas** (which makes a pause when you read it) after the words 'I own this'?

5 In the first stanza there is a list of places. In the second stanza there is a list of things that happen. What direction does the list in the second stanza move in, compared to the first?

6 How does the writer make the things in the second stanza seem bigger and more active? Think about:
   • the number of words she uses
   • the language devices she uses, such as **personification** – giving non-human things like trees human characteristics.

7 a What does the word 'proclaiming' mean?
   b What does the use of this word suggest to you about man's state of mind when he does something like climbing a mountain and planting a flag?

Words/phrases to explore (AO1 and AO2)

ACTIVITY 2

1 What can you say about the last line?

2 What do you think 'the other way round' means?

3 How does the **structure** of the poem mirror 'the other way round'? Think about what the voices say as well as the change of direction in the poem.

Cold Knap Lake

by Gillian Clarke

Read the poem in your AQA
Anthology, then complete the
activities below.

Initial responses

1   a   What happens in the first three **stanzas** of the poem?
    b   Who are the different people involved in the story?

2   The first three stanzas are written from the point of view of a child.
    How does the poet show that it is a child's viewpoint? Think about
    the words she uses, and how she describes her mother.

3   'My mother gave a stranger's child her breath.' What is the mother
    doing here, and how is this clearly her child's point of view?

4   'Was I there?' comes after a gap, and is the shortest line in the
    poem.
    a   Why is this question a surprise when you read it? Think about
        what it looks like when you look at the whole poem on the page.
    b   How does the time of the poem alter at this point? Think about
        the age of 'I'.

5   The sentences in the fourth stanza are questions.
    a   What is the **speaker** uncertain about?
    b   Which words in the stanza suggest uncertainty, or things being
        lost?

6   There are some **echoes** and **half-rhymes** in the poem, but the only
    full **rhyme** in the poem is formed by the last two lines.
    a   Why do you think the poet decided to do this?
    b   What things is she joining together by using rhyme?

Words/phrases to explore (A01 and A02)

The last two lines seem almost like part of a nursery rhyme. What else
in the poem seems to be like a children's story, and what seems very
adult?

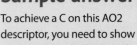

GradeStudio

Sample answer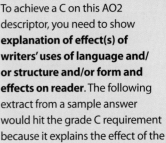

To achieve a C on this AO2
descriptor, you need to show
**explanation of effect(s) of
writers' uses of language and/
or structure and/or form and
effects on reader.** The following
extract from a sample answer
would hit the grade C requirement
because it explains the effect of the
pause in the poem.

> The pause created by
> the comma after 'the
> child breathed' lets the
> reader take in that it
> has actually been saved.
> Up to that point you
> think that it died.

Price We Pay for the Sun

by Grace Nichols

Read the poem in your AQA Anthology, then complete the activities below.

Initial responses   ACTIVITY 1

1   In the poem as a whole, what is good about the islands and what isn't? Find evidence to support what you think.

2   Who do you think the 'we' and 'you' in the poem might be? Support your answer with evidence.

3   Why does Nichols repeat the word 'real'? Think about what isn't 'real'.

4   The writer compares the islands to the people who live there. Which phrase in the first **stanza** is the first to make a comparison?

5   What features of the islands that are not like 'picture postcards' are mentioned in the second stanza?

6   How are these features compared to bad things happening to the **speaker's** family?

7   a   Nichols invents a word, 'sulph-furious', to describe her mother's cancer. What other words does this word come from?
    b   What is she saying about the illness? Remember that she is comparing the islands' features to the inhabitants.

Words/phrases to explore (AO1 and AO2)   ACTIVITY 2

Look at the last three lines of the poem and the first three. What is Nichols saying about the islands overall?

Neighbours

by Gillian Clarke

Read the poem in your AQA Anthology, then complete the activities below.

Initial responses

ACTIVITY 1

1 'That spring was late'. What other signs are there in the first **stanza** that there iws something wrong in nature?

2 Go through the poem and jot down all the other examples you can find of things being 'wrong'.

3 'A mouthful of bitter air' (fourth stanza). Why is the air described as 'bitter'? Try to think of more than one reason.

4 What does the 'box of sorrows' refer to? Read the 'Context' above again if you're not sure.

5 Why is the rain described as a 'poisoned arrow'? Think about both words.

6 What exactly do you think the writer means by 'neighbourly' in the sixth stanza? Think about where the places in the poem are, and personal relationships – what 'neighbours' means. Where can you find both ideas in this stanza?

7 Why are they looking for a bird 'with green in its voice'? Think of the various associations with the word 'green'.

Words/phrases to explore (AO1 and AO2)

ACTIVITY 2

Analyse the last three lines.

1 Why do you think the writer uses two other languages here?

2 What does the 'break of blue' imply? Think of as many reasons as you can.

3 Why do you think the lines are shorter here than in the rest of the poem? Look at the shape of the clines on the page.

GradeStudio

Context

The **Chernobyl disaster** was a nuclear reactor accident in 1986 in Ukraine. It resulted in the release of radioactivity into the atmosphere over a wide area, which affected human beings, birds, animals and food production.

▶ **Poem Glossary**

isobars lines of atmospheric pressure on a map, which might suggest wind direction

fjords narrow sea inlets on the Norwegian coast

gall poisonous bitter liquid

caesium a dangerous element released into the atmosphere from the disaster

democracy a system of government where everybody has an equal vote

glasnost (Russian) open process of government (a word associated with the liberalisation of the Soviet Union in the late 1980s)

golau glas (Welsh) blue light

GradeStudio

Sample answer

To achieve a C on this AO1 descriptor, you need to show **effective use of details.** The following extract from a sample answer would hit the grade C requirement:

The poem is full of poison – 'gall', 'bitter air', 'the poisoned arrow', and a lamb that 'sips caesium' rather than clean milk.

43

Crossing the Loch

by Kathleen Jamie

Read the poem in your AQA Anthology, then complete the activities below.

Initial responses

ACTIVITY 1

1   What happens during the poem? Look at the first and last lines, and then pick out the facts of what happens in between these two moments.

2   The first word of the poem is 'Remember'. Look through the rest of the poem and jot down all the words and phrases that remind the reader that this is a poem of memory – what is remembered and what is forgotten.

3   At the end of the first **stanza**, how does the writer use the idea of a mouth to describe the start of the journey?

4   Look at the second stanza.
    a   What dangers are mentioned or suggested in the stanza? Look at the words used.
    b   How does the writer use the senses of hearing and touch to capture the feelings of the people in the boat? Think about what they can hear, what they can feel, and how it affects them.

5   In the third stanza, how is the boat 'like a twittering nest'? Think about both words and what the people and the boat look and sound like.

6   How is the boat like a 'small boat of saints'? Think of the effect of the phosphorescence.

7   Why is the bow wave like a 'magic dart'? Think about the phosphorescence again.

GradeStudio

Sample answer **E**

To achieve an E on this AO1 descriptor, you need to show **supported response to text**. The following extract from a sample answer would hit the grade E requirement.

> Activity 1, question 7
> The journey across the loch seemed like magic.

To move to the D band, you would have to **explain** why it seemed like magic.

Words/phrases to explore (A02)

ACTIVITY 2

1   What has happened to the people in the boat since that night? Read the last stanza carefully.

2   Why do you think they remember this small event? Write a few sentences on this, remembering to give evidence for your answer.

Hard Water

by Jean Sprackland

Read the poem in your AQA Anthology, then complete the activities below.

▶ Poem Glossary

hard water contains more dissolved minerals than soft water; it is good for brewing, but makes soap less effective. The minerals such as limestone and gypsum make it taste sharper, and help to form limescale in kettles

hey up me duck a familiar greeting in the Midlands. The poet was brought up in Burton-upon-Trent, which is famous for brewing beer

alchemical taste the taste of a chemical which transforms onr thing into something else

mardy a Midlands word for sulky

Initial responses

ACTIVITY 1

1 What is it about the water and her home town that the **speaker** likes? Go through the poem looking for the words and phrases that tell you this, and make a note of them.

2 a The first three lines are about a holiday experience. Why do you think there is a break after these lines?
  b What do you think has happened during the pause here.

3 What do you think the 'little fizz of anxiety' is? Think about the water and how the speaker is feeling.

4 'It couldn't lie.' What does the water tell the truth about? Look at the next two sentences.

5 Look at the four lines beginning 'I let a different cleverness'.
  a The writer has 'book-learning', but what is the 'cleverness' of her home city? What are people like there?
  b How do these four lines use the idea of water? Look carefully at all the words.

6 Who do you think might have said 'too bloody deep for me', and why?

7 The writer is marked as 'belonging, regardless'. What does she belong to, do you think, and 'regardless' of what?

Words/phrases to explore (AO1 and AO2)

ACTIVITY 2

Remind yourself of the words 'Flat. Straight.'

1 What do these two words apply to? Think of more than one thing.

2 How does the way the words are written add to the effect?

GradeStudio

Sample answer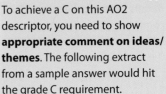

To achieve a C on this AO2 descriptor, you need to show **appropriate comment on ideas/ themes**. The following extract from a sample answer would hit the grade C requirement.

> **Activity 1, question 1**
> The speaker has several attitudes to the water. She doesn't always seem to like it, because it's 'not quite clean' and the rain falls with a 'payload of acid', but in the end she seems to love it, as she sees it as 'fierce lovely water'.

London

by William Blake

Read the poem in your AQA Anthology, then complete the activities below.

ACTIVITY 1

Initial responses

1 Make a list of all the people the **speaker** sees in the streets of London. What do they all have in common?

2 Look through the whole poem, and pick out all the words that suggest grief, danger, destruction or cruelty.

3 There are a lot of repetitions of words in the poem.
   a Go through the poem carefully and make a note of them.
   b What is the overall effect of having so many repetitions, do you think?

4 'Marks of weakness, marks of woe'. What 'marks' do you think the speaker sees?

5 Look at the phrase 'mind-forged manacles'.
   a In what ways are the people in the city tied?
   b Work out what the term 'mind-forged' means. How are their bonds 'mind-forged'?

6 a What were working conditions like for early nineteenth-century chimney sweeps? (You might need to do some research to help you here.)
   b How might their cries 'appal' the church? Think what the church stands for.

7 In Blake's picture of London, everything that should be innocent or happy is not. Find three examples of this in the last few lines.

ACTIVITY 2

Words/phrases to explore (AO1 and AO2)

Of all the things that the speaker sees in London, which does he think is the worst? Which do you think is the worst? Write this down, giving reasons for your answers.

GradeStudio

Sample answer D

To achieve a D on this AO1 descriptor, you need to use **details to support a range of comments**. The following extract from a sample answer would hit the grade D requirement.

> **Activity 2**
> Everybody in the poem seems to be unhappy, full of 'woe'. The children live in 'fear', the chimney sweepers 'cry', and the reader is also invited to feel sorry for the soldier's 'sigh'. The worst thing is not simply that the prostitutes are young, but that they even 'curse' their own babies.

The Prelude (extract)

by William Wordsworth

Read the poem in your AQA Anthology, then complete the activities below.

Initial responses

ACTIVITY 1

1 Write down exactly what the boy does in this extract from 'The Prelude', and why he does it.

2 a What evidence is there to suggest that the boy feels guilty for what he does? Look at the first eight lines of the extract.
  b How does his guilt come back again later in the poem?

3 The **speaker** describes the circles behind the boat melting 'into one track'. How does this suggest the distance the boat travels? Think about it from the boy's point of view in the boat.

4 Read the lines from 'But now' to 'like a swan' (lines 11–20). How does Wordsworth suggest that the boy enjoys the place and the activity in these lines? Think about what the boy does and what he sees.

5 Look at the lines from 'When, from behind' to 'Strode after me.' (lines 21–29). The mountains suddenly seem threatening. How does Wordsworth achieve this? Think about:
  a the ways the mountains are **personified** (made to seem living)
  b the adjectives used to describe the mountains.

6 The boy's mood has changed from the opening. He has two responses to what happens. What is his immediate response (look at the lines from 'With trembling oars' to 'serious mood'), and what does he think about it later (look at the last 10 lines)?

Words/phrases to explore (AO1 and AO2)

ACTIVITY 2

Choose the line that you think best captures:
• the boy's enjoyment of rowing • his mood at the end of the poem.
Compare the differences in the lines – not just the feelings, but how Wordsworth creates them by the ways he writes the lines.

The Wild Swans at Coole

by W. B. Yeats

Read the poem in your AQA Anthology, then complete the activities below.

▶ **Poem Glossary**

clamorous noisy

> Activity 2
>
> The speaker admires and delights in the swans, which he describes as 'beautiful' 'brilliant creatures'. He admires their long life and constancy as they rise 'lover by lover' from the stream and fly, and they are 'unwearied', by time and perhaps by each other.

Initial responses

ACTIVITY 1

1. a. How long is it since the **speaker** first saw the swans?
   b. What exactly does he see them do when he's watching them?

2. The first **stanza** seems very still. Which words make it seem still?

3. The second stanza seems very active. Which words make it seem active?

4. Lines 4 and 10 are both short.
   a. How does line 4 add to the effect of stillness?
   b. How does line 10 add to the sense of action?

5. In the third stanza, the speaker's heart is 'sore'.
   a. Why, do you think? What do the swans make him think of?
   b. What might have changed?

6. a. In the fourth stanza, how do the swans seem unchanged?
   b. How might the speaker have changed, unlike the swans?

7. Why does Yeats choose to end the poem with a question? Think about the effect.

Words/phrases to explore (AO1 and AO2)

ACTIVITY 2

What is the effect of the swans on the speaker? Think about what he tells you about his mood, and how he describes the swans.

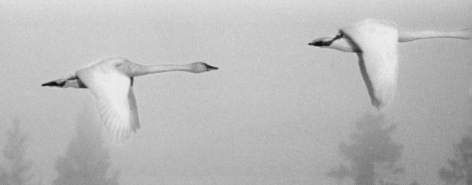

Spellbound

by Emily Brontë

Read the poem in your AQA Anthology, then complete the activities below.

Initial responses

ACTIVITY 1

1 a Looking at the poem as a whole, what can the **speaker** not do?

   b Why do you think she feels like this? Support what you think with some details from the poem.

2 The speaker thinks she is under a spell, and describes it as a 'tyrant' spell. Why does she use this word to describe it?

3 What is the effect of repeating 'cannot' at the end of the first **stanza**? What does it tell you about how the speaker feels?

4 Which words in the second stanza make the weather seem more threatening?

5 What do the first two lines of the last stanza say about how the speaker feels?

6 Look at the last line of the poem. Which words tell you that the speaker's determination not to move has strengthened from the first stanza?

Words/phrases to explore (AO1 and AO2)

ACTIVITY 2

How does the writer make you realise what the speaker's mental state is? Look for repetitions of words and sounds in lines, between lines, and between stanzas.

You could start by working on 'wastes beyond wastes below'. Try writing a paragraph about her mental state and how it is shown, starting from this line.

▶ **Poem Glossary**

drear dreary, gloomy

tyrant a ruler owho exercises absolute power

GradeStudio

Sample answer **B**

To achieve a B on this AO1 descriptor, you need to show **considered/qualified response to text**. The following extract from a sample answer would hit the grade B requirement.

> Activity 1, question 6
> The speaker in the poem seems terrified by the conditions, as shown by adjectives such as 'wild' and 'giant', so that she is unable to move; but 'I will not' in the last line suggests something else is going on in her mind beyond mere terror.

Below the Green Corrie
by Norman McCaig

Read the poem in your AQA Anthology, then complete the activities below.

GradeStudio

Sample answer Ⓓ

To achieve a D on this AO2 descriptor, you need to show **identification of effect(s) of writer's choices of language.** To do this, you need to identify the effect of a device, not simply name it. The following extract from a sample answer would hit the grade D requirement:

> Activity 1, question 7b
> The metaphor 'a bandolier of light' in the last line of the poem describes the shaft of sunlight hitting the mountain, so the speaker feels better about the experience at the end.

To move to C, you would have to explain exactly why the line gives 'a better feeling'.

ACTIVITY 1

Initial responses

1 What is the **speaker** doing in the mountains and what exactly does he see and hear? Find evidence for what you think.

2 The mountains are personified (made to seem like living things) right through the poem, beginning with 'like bandits'. Find some other examples of **personification** in the poem.

3 'Full of threats'. Which other words and phrases suggest threat in the first **stanza**?

4 a Why do you think 'full of' is repeated in line 4?
  b What effect does it have?

5 What do you associate the phrases 'stand and deliver' and 'your money or your life' with? How does this fit with the ideas in the first stanza?

6 The weather is 'ugly'.
  a What exactly is the weather like? Refer to details in the poem.
  b How does the weather seem to change in the poem?

7 a What is 'a bandolier of light'?
  b Why do you think McCaig chooses this as the last phrase of the poem?

ACTIVITY 2

Words/phrases to explore (AO1 and AO2)

1 'My life was enriched/with an infusion of theirs'. How do you think the poet's life has been 'enriched' by the experience?

2 Why do you think the first five words are on a line of their own?

Storm in the Black Forest

by D. H. Lawrence

Read the poem in your AQA Anthology, then complete the
activities below.

Initial responses

1 What exactly does the **speaker** see and hear in the poem? What
time of day is it?

2 Look at the nine words beginning 'white liquid'.
   a Which vowel sound is repeated again and again here? (This is
      called **assonance**.)
   b Why do you think the writer does this? Think about what is
      being described.
   c Now look at the whole two lines beginning 'jugfull'. What other
      repetitions are there?

3 a 'and is gone' describes the disappearance of the lightning. What
      sound has disappeared with it? Think about the work you did in
      answering the last question.
   b Why do you think the writer puts 'and is gone' on a separate
      line? What does it emphasise, and how?

4 In line 7 the writer compares the lightning to a 'white snake'. What
other words does he use to compare the lightning to a snake?

5 Look at line 9. What words are used to suggest the storm is
something inhuman?

6 There are three exclamation marks in the last four lines. Why do
you think the writer does this?

Words/phrases to explore (AO1 and AO2)

Do you think the speaker here admires the storm? Find specific
evidence for what you think.

▶ **Poem Glossary**

subjugated subdued

uncouth rude, strange

GradeStudio

Sample answer D

To achieve a D on this AO1
descriptor, you need to show
**explained response to
element(s) of text**. The following
extract from a sample answer
would hit the grade D requirement.

Activity 2
It's clear that the
speaker admires the
lightning particularly,
because he describes
it as 'pure', 'white' and
'gold-bronze', and
he admires its power,
because it can't be
'subjugated' by man.

Wind

by Ted Hughes

Read the poem in your AQA Anthology, then complete the activities below.

GradeStudio

Sample answer C

To achieve a C on this AO2 descriptor, you need to show **explanation of effect(s) of writers' uses of language and/or structure and/or form and effects on reader**. To do this, you need to work hard on your view of the ideas in the poem. The following extract from a sample answer would hit the grade C requirement.

Activity 1, question 4

The word 'scaled' makes it sound like it's as difficult as climbing a mountain when the speaker just walks along the side of the house, so you realise how strong the wind was to make him struggle in that way.

Initial responses
ACTIVITY 1

1   In the whole poem, how are the people aware of the power of the wind? Think about what they see and hear and feel.

2   **a**   What is the house being compared to in the first line?
    b   What other two things is it compared to in the last two **stanzas**?

3   Jot down all the action words in the first stanza, such as 'crashing'. What things here are made to seem alive, which aren't usually?

4   How does the writer suggest the strength of the wind in the third stanza? Look for at least three things.

5   Why do you think the fields seem to be 'quivering'? Remember that the **speaker** is looking at the view in front of him.

6   In the last stanza, inanimate things are **personified** again – given living qualities, as in the first stanza. How many can you find? Jot them down.

Words/phrases to explore (AO1 and AO2)
ACTIVITY 2

Which line of the poem best shows the power of the storm? Look for a line which you can say at least two things about, including something about the way the line is written that makes it powerful.

Looking at the poems individually: what have you learned?

My learning ▶

In this section you will:
- think about which poems interested you most and why.

Complete Activities 1 and 2 below. As you do, think about which poems and which features of poems were most interesting to you.

Note that the words in bold in the tasks below refer to the key words in the Assessment Objectives.

Assessment Objective 1 (AO1)

ACTIVITY 1

1 Which of these poems did you **respond** to most strongly? You may have liked it, or disliked it, or found it the most interesting, or horrible. You may have a number of things to say about it.
   Working with a partner, or by yourself, display your responses as a spider diagram, and then compare it with someone else's, to see if you have responded to the poems in similar ways.

2 Which poems did you find it easiest to offer an **interpretation** about? In other words, you had an opinion about a poem's meaning that you could argue from the text and **select detail** to support your opinion. For instance, you might have found it easy to argue and support the view that the speaker in 'Spellbound' is suffering a breakdown.
   Suggesting more than one interpretation of a poem, or parts of a poem, gives you opportunities to score more marks. For instance, there are several ways in which you could interpret the nature of the mountains in the excerpt from 'The Prelude'.

Assessment Objective 2 (AO2)

ACTIVITY 2

1 Which features of **language**, **structure** or **form** did you understand best? The most promising ones to write about in the exam will be the ones where you have most to say. For instance, you might have found several things to say about:
   - the effect of personification in 'Below the Green Corrie' (**language**)
   - the way 'A Vision' changes at the end (**structure**)
   - the effects of the change to full rhyme at the end of 'Cold Knap Lake' (**form**).

2 What **ideas** did you pick out in the poems? Again, the best answers will probably identify more than one idea in a poem, or several aspects of one idea. For instance, you might have identified or explored more than one idea about society in 'London'.

My learning ▶

In this section you will learn how to:
- compare poems and address the Assessment Objectives
- develop writing skills and practise exam-style questions.

Comparing the 'Place' poems

Assessment Objective 3 is broken into two parts:

▶ comparing ideas and themes in the poems, with detail

▶ comparing the ways writers use language or structure or form, with detail.

In responding to the exam question, you will need to address both these parts.

Assessment Objective:

The Assessment Objective you will be focusing on in this part of the chapter is:

 AO3 make comparisons and explain links between texts, evaluating writers' different ways of expressing meaning and achieving effects.

Comparing ideas and themes

Read the poems 'Hard Water' and 'London' then complete the activities below.

ACTIVITY 1

Think about the ideas and themes in the two poems. List as many similarities and differences as you can. Both poems are about particular places. Think about:
- whether the places have anything in common
- whether the attitudes to the places in the poems are similar or different.

ACTIVITY 2

Using your list of similarities and differences from Activity 1, decide how different each of the poems are for each point you made. For example, the **speaker** in 'London' seems to dislike the place. How can you tell this from the details of the poem? The speaker in 'Hard Water', loved coming 'home'. What exactly does she love? Does she have any other emotions about it? Are any of them like anything in 'London'?

Use quotations or refer to specific parts of the poem to support what you think.

ACTIVITY 3

Compare the differences in the ways the poems are written. For example, the two poems are very different in the ways they are written, but they are both first person poems, which is a starting point in itself.
- The language of the two poems is very different, because they were written at different times. How is the language of one poem modern, and the other not? Be as exact as you can about this – don't just stop at "London' has lots of old words'. Note down some exact details.
- Which of the five senses (seeing, hearing, touching, tasting and smelling) does each poem use? Remember you're looking for similarities and differences.
- 'London' uses lots of rhyme and repetition to create effects. What does 'Hard Water' use? Think about the sound of some of the words, and the breaks between lines.

Comparing writers' methods

One of the best ways to score well when comparing poems is to compare two details, one from each poem, that you can say a lot about when you put them together. Find a detail from each poem that you could compare directly. For example:

> And mark in every face I meet
> Marks of weakness, marks of woe
>
> (London)

> It tasted of work, the true taste
> Of early mornings, the blunt taste
> Of don't get mardy, of too bloody deep for me
> Fierce lovely water that marked me for life
> As belonging, regardless.
>
> (Hard Water)

You could say that both of the speakers meet people who they don't seem to like very much, but that would only be a simple link between the details, which is in the F band of marks. What more can you find to say? Think about:

- Which of these seems more damning about the place? Which words tell you this, and which words tell you that the attitude in the other poem is quite different?
- 'London' seems to have one attitude to the people in this extract, but 'Hard Water' seems to have more than one. What are they?
- Which senses are used in these extracts?

GradeStudio

Sample answer E

To achieve a grade E on this AO3 descriptor, you need to make **some comment(s) on similarities/differences, with detail**. The following extract from a sample answer to Activity 4 would hit the grade E requirement.

> Both poems use the senses to convey the attitudes about the place. 'London' uses sight, such as 'mark every face I meet', whereas 'Hard Water' uses taste, such as 'It tasted of work'.

GradeStudio

Sample answer D

To achieve a grade D on this AO3 descriptor, you need to make some **structured comments on similarities/differences, with detail**. The following extract from a sample answer to activity 4 would hit the grade D requirement.

> Both poems use the senses to convey the attitudes about the place. 'London' uses sight, such as 'mark every face I meet', whereas 'Hard Water' uses taste, such as 'It tasted of work'. They both use hearing, though. The speaker in 'London' hears 'in every voice ... the mind-forged manacles'. Hearing in 'Hard Water' is implied rather than said, but 'don't get mardy' and 'too bloody deep for me' are obviously things said to the speaker.

Putting it all together

To practise the skills you have been working on in these comparison activities, here are four more questions on a different pair of poems: 'Below the Green Corrie' and the extract from 'The Prelude'.

1 What ideas and themes can you find in the poems which are similar?
   a Both the poems are about people alone in a natural surrounding. What attitudes to nature can you find in the poems?
   b What similarities and differences are there in the type of threat that nature seems to make?
   c What are the effects on the **speakers** of their experiences? List as many similarities and differences as you can.

2 Now you need to think about how the poems are written.
   a Both poems use **personification** – they write about the mountains as though they are living. Find some examples in each, and jot them down.
   b Both poems change in mood. Find the words in each poem that best express the two moods in each, and jot them down. Then look at them to see if you can find some similarities or differences.
   c These are both first person poems, but only one of them tells you very specifically about his feelings. How does Wordsworth convey his feelings? Look for some details. Now look for any signs of feelings in 'Below the Green Corrie', and decide if there are any similarities or differences.

3 Now you have a list of similarities and differences between the two poems, you can consider how similar they are, or how different. For instance, the mountains seem to threaten both speakers, but how different are the threats? Do the threats stay or not? For how long? Include some detail or evidence to support each point.

4 Find a detail from each poem that you could compare directly, for example:

The simple link between the two details above is that they both describe the mountains apparently moving towards the speakers. However, to reach the

> Their leader
> swaggered up close in the dark light
> full of threats, full of thunders.

(Below the Green Corrie)

> with purpose of its own
> And measured motion like a living thing
> Strode after me.

(The Prelude)

grades you are aiming for, you need to explore all the similarities and differences you can find between the details. So here you would need to consider:
* Which seems more threatening, and why?
* What type of movement does each seem to make?
* How do the speakers in each poem seem to react to the movement?
* How does each detail fit into the poems as a whole?

Now you could write a paragraph, or more, comparing the details. Try it!

GradeStudio

Sample answer

To achieve a grade C on this AO3 descriptor, you need to show **sustained focus on similarities/ differences** with material for a range of comparisons. The following extract from a sample answer would hit the grade C requirement.

> The mountains in both poems seem threatening. In 'Green Corrie' they are 'full of threats, full of thunders' and in 'The Prelude' the huge peak has a 'grim shape', and appears to follow the boy rowing. There is a sense of being surrounded in both poems, too, as the mountains 'gathered round me' ('Green Corrie') and 'Towered up between me and the stars' ('Prelude'). The feeling of the poems is very different, though. The threat of the mountains in 'Green Corrie' is over after line 4. After that, they seem to give to the speaker, rather than the other way around, and he feels that his life is 'enriched' by them. It is the other way round in 'The Prelude'. At the beginning the boy is sort of enriched by the pleasure he gets when he is rowing on the lake, and he is 'proud of his skill', but when the mountains suddenly threaten him it goes on right to the end of the poem.

GradeStudio

Sample answer

To achieve a grade B on this AO3 descriptor, you need to make a **developed comparison of writers' uses of language and/or structure and/or form and effects on readers, with detail**. If the following paragraph was added to the one above, it would easily hit the grade B requirement.

> The personification in both poems suggests that the mountains are powerful and aggressive, as well as just threatening. They are 'like bandits' that 'swaggered', and they 'gathered round me' ('Below the Green Corrie') and in 'The Prelude' they have 'voluntary power' and 'Strode after me'. These are different types of personification, though. In 'Below the Green Corrie' the comparison is very specific. The mountains are described as 'bandits' throughout: they were 'prowlers' who 'swaggered' wearing a 'bandolier' and 'swashbuckling'. Wordsworth is not as specific as this, and the mountains seem more threatening because they are unknown. They are 'like a living thing' and 'unknown modes of being', 'mighty forms'.

ACTIVITY 6

Comparing writers' methods and purposes

Compare the ways in which the two writers personify the mountains.

Think about:

- what each **personification** suggests about the mountains
- what different sorts of threats are suggested
- how the personifications create different **tones** in the poem.

My learning ▶

In this section you will learn how to:
● structure a response in the exam
● use the skills you have learned to perform successfully.

Assessment Objectives:

 A01 respond to texts critically and imaginatively; select and evaluate relevant textual detail to illustrate and support interpretations.

 A02 explain how language, structure and form contribute to writers' presentation of ideas, themes and settings.

 A03 make comparisons and explain links between texts, evaluating writers' different ways of expressing meaning and achieving effects.

Writing in the exam

Planning and writing your response

When faced with any exam question your approach should be.

Read

Read the questions – what exactly are you being asked to do? The questions should remind you about the Assessment Objectives. There will be a choice of two questions, so you need to make a choice quickly. Each question will ask you to compare a named poem with an unnamed poem, so your choice might be based on the poem that is named, or on what each question is asking you to do.

Think

This is the planning stage. The first word of the exam task is likely to be 'compare'. One of the descriptors in the mark band for a grade C is 'sustained focus on similarities/differences'. This suggests that a wise course of action would be to build your response around a comparison of the two poems.

This doesn't mean that everything you write should be comparative. Rather, you should decide how you're going to compare the poems before you write. Use a plan like the one on page 60. Within that, you need to jot down quickly some of the ideas from the poems, and perhaps one or two details that you're planning to use – you should choose things that you can write quite a lot about.

The thinking is more important than the writing here. The whole process might take 5 minutes, perhaps (certainly not less than 2 minutes). You only have 45 minutes for the whole task. Don't start writing straight away, think about the question carefully first!

Write

When you write, what you are going to show is:

▶ what you think about the poems

▶ why they are written in the ways that they are

▶ what happens when you compare the poems, or parts of them.

In other words, these are the things the Assessment Objectives focus on. The phrase 'or parts of them', is important. No question will ask you to write down everything you know about the poems. You have to select from what you know to think and write about the poems in answer to this question, in the ways that you've practised as you've worked through this section.

Edit

If you have any time left, you should look for ways to improve your answer. Don't look for spelling or punctuation errors: these don't carry marks here. Could you quickly add another possible meaning of a word or phrase that you've written about? Is there another idea about the effect of a writer's choice of language? Additions of this kind might gain you an extra mark.

Putting it into practice

Let's take a typical exam question:

Compare (AO3) the ways in which weather (AO1) is presented (AO2) in 'Storm in the Black Forest' and one other poem from 'Place'.

Let's suppose that you chose 'Wind' as a good poem to compare with 'Storm in the Black Forest' – both are about storms, use a range of devices, and deal with a relationship between humans and nature, though they are very different.

First, jot down a few ideas from the poems that you're going to use when you write. For example:

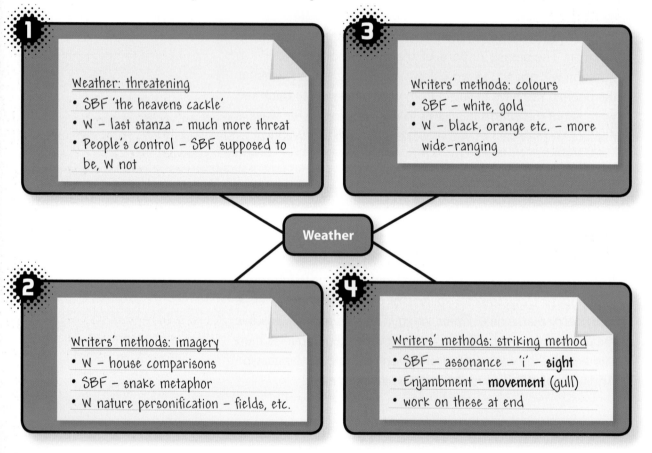

1

Weather: threatening
• SBF 'the heavens cackle'
• W – last stanza – much more threat
• People's control – SBF supposed to be, W not

3

Writers' methods: colours
• SBF – white, gold
• W – black, orange etc. – more wide-ranging

Weather

2

Writers' methods: imagery
• W – house comparisons
• SBF – snake metaphor
• W nature personification – fields, etc.

4

Writers' methods: striking method
• SBF – assonance – 'i' – **sight**
• Enjambment – **movement** (gull)
• work on these at end

In the notes above, the student decided that the weather in each poem was very threatening, so that might be a good place to start, but the poems were very different in method, so the rest of the response could be structured around different methods. Three ideas about method is plenty: the task is not to try to offer an exhaustive account – you are just showing off your thinking and writing skills.

After thinking of the three methods, the student planned which order to write about the methods in (indicated by the numbers). Having chosen this structure, the student thought that an opening paragraph showing what she was going to say would help the reader. Often this is unnecessary, but here she could start work on all three Assessment Objectives quickly.

Read the extracts from these sample student answers, together with the question below and the examiner comments. You could then try the sample exam question on page 63.

Compare the ways in which weather is presented in 'Storm in the Black Forest' and one other poem from 'Place'.

Openings

E grade answer

Student A

The weather presented in these poems seems very similar, in some ways. It is extreme, with huge amounts of lightning in 'Storm in the Black Forest' and a wind that seems like a hurricane in 'Wind'. There are lots of comparisons in both poems.

Examiner comment

Student A has made **a comment on similarity** (E), with some **support** (E) by mentioning the types of weather, and there is **simple identification of method** (F).

D grade answer

Student B

The weather presented in these poems seems very similar, in some ways. It is extreme, with huge amounts of lightning in 'Storm in the Black Forest' and a wind that seems like a hurricane in 'Wind'. Both situations seem very threatening, but much more so in 'Wind', where the human beings are terrified. In 'Storm in the Black Forest' they are not so much terrified as amazed. The methods used by the poets are similar in some ways, with a lot of comparisons, but they use other techniques as well.

Examiner comment

Student B does a little better, by making some **structured comment on similarity** (D) and difference, though unsupported. She also indicates that she is going to deal with more than one method.

Examiner comment

Both these openings start to achieve in the Assessment Objectives, by comparing the poems in terms of what they are about and how they are written. Of course what both students eventually achieve depends on what they write in the rest of the responses. They must not repeat what they've written here, though. It is worth noting that they could not have written their subsequent paragraphs without doing the thinking shown in these openings first.

GradeStudio

A paragraph on an idea

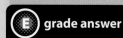

Student A

'Wind' is a lot more threatening than 'Storm in the Black Forest'. The house seems to have been 'far out at sea all night', and the people in the house 'grip our hearts', meaning that they are nervous about what's happening outside. You don't know what the people watching the lightning feel, though the sky 'cackles with an uncouth sound', which makes it sound nasty.

Examiner comment

Student A **supports the response** (E) of the weather being threatening, and provides a **comment on detail** (E) about 'grip our hearts'. There is also **some comment on similarity** (E), **with support** (E), so four of the six descriptors in the E band are hit just in these two sentences.

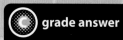

Student B

'Wind' is a lot more threatening than 'Storm in the Black Forest'. The house being 'far out at sea all night' suggests that it has been in danger, and words like 'crashing', 'booming' and 'stampeding' all suggest something violent happening. The light is described as 'Blade-light', which gives the idea that the wind makes the flashing light as sharp as a knife when it hits your eyes. The people in the house seem to be terrified at the end, because they 'grip' their hearts, which tells you how nervous they feel, and when they 'feel the roots of the house move' they must feel that the whole place is shaking, which must be really frightening.

Examiner comment

Student B's paragraph here is just about one poem, with a **simple link** (F) at the beginning, but she went on to write the next paragraph about the other poem, comparing as she went. Here she has a **range of comments on details** (D), and **awareness of feelings** (D) about the people in the house. She also **identifies the effect** (D) of the list of words, and gives an **explanation of the effect** (C) of 'Blade-light'.

A paragraph comparing two details

 grade answer

Student A

Both poems use comparisons to convey what they have to say. In 'Wind' the house is compared to a 'fine green goblet', and the lightning in 'Storm in the Black Forest' is also compared to a container with 'jugfull after jugfull' of light.

Examiner comment

Student A makes a **comment on similarity** (E) **with support** (E) and **shows awareness of the writers' choices** (E), but does not **identify the effect** (D) of either of the comparisons.

 grade answer

Student B

Both poems use comparisons to convey what they have to say. In 'Wind' the house is compared to a 'fine green goblet' because it rings with the force of the wind on it, and it's so strong that it seems as though it will shatter like a glass. 'Fine' makes it seem fragile, which adds to the idea of danger, and a 'goblet' perhaps suggests something precious which is about to be lost. The lightning in 'Storm in the Black Forest' is compared to a snake, which also has associations of danger, and again there is sound involved, as the heavens 'cackle with uncouth sounds'.

Examiner comment

Student B has some **structured comment** (D) **with support** (D), but does really well with 'fine green goblet'. She clearly **explains the effect** (C) of the phrase, but by adding the ideas about the glass being fragile and precious she moves to **appreciation of writer's use of language** (B).

You are now ready to tackle an exam question. Here's one to try:

Compare the unpleasant effects of nature shown in 'Neighbours' and one other poem from 'Place'.

When you've written your answer, you could mark it, or get a partner to mark it, using the mark scheme on page 142.

Further comparison activities

Below are some comparison activities that you could attempt for each of the poems in the 'Place' cluster.

The Blackbird of Glanmore

1 **Comparing ideas and themes**
Compare the relationship between humans and nature in 'The Blackbird of Glanmore' and 'The Wild Swans at Coole'.

2 **Comparing writers' devices**
Compare the ways in which the writers use **structure** in 'The Blackbird of Glanmore' and 'The Wild Swans at Coole'.

A Vision

1 **Comparing ideas and themes**
Compare the views of society shown in 'A Vision' and 'London'.

2 **Comparing writers' devices**
Compare how the writers of 'A Vision' and 'Wind' capture the mood of the poems in the opening lines.

The Moment

1 **Comparing ideas and themes**
Compare the relationship between man and nature in 'The Moment' and 'Wind'.

2 **Comparing writers' devices**
Compare the ways in which the writers of 'The Moment' and 'Wind' suggest the power of nature.

Cold Knap Lake

1 **Comparing ideas and themes**
Compare the effects of memory in 'Cold Knap Lake' and 'The Wild Swans at Coole'.

2 **Comparing writers' devices**
Compare how Gillian Clarke shapes the endings of 'Cold Knap Lake' and 'Neighbours' to affect the reader.

Price We Pay for the Sun

1 **Comparing ideas and themes**
Compare how the reality of a place is shown in 'Price We Pay for the Sun' and 'Hard Water'.

2 **Comparing writers' devices**
Compare how a place is made to seem unpleasant in 'Price We Pay for the Sun' and 'London'.

Neighbours

1 **Comparing ideas and themes**
Compare the unpleasant aspects of nature shown in 'Neighbours' and 'Price We Pay for the Sun'.

2 **Comparing writers' devices**
Compare the effects of the endings of 'Neighbours' and 'Cold Knap Lake'.

Crossing the Loch

1 **Comparing ideas and themes**
Compare the experiences of rowing at night in 'Crossing the Loch' and 'The Prelude'.

2 **Comparing writers' devices**
Compare the ways in which the writers describe rowing in 'Crossing the Loch' and 'The Prelude'.

Hard Water

1 **Comparing ideas and themes**
Compare the feelings of the speakers in 'Hard Water' and 'A Vision'.

2 **Comparing writers' devices**
Compare the ways in which the writers use the senses in 'Hard Water' and 'Wind'.

London

1 **Comparing ideas and themes**
Compare the ways things are destroyed in 'London' and 'Wind'.

2 **Comparing writers' devices**
Compare how the writers of 'London' and 'Price We Pay for the Sun' make a place seem unpleasant.

The Prelude

1 **Comparing ideas and themes**
Compare what the writers say about the countryside in 'The Prelude' and 'Below the Green Corrie'.

2 **Comparing writers' devices**
Compare the ways in which the writers of 'The Prelude' and 'Below the Green Corrie' describe the mountains.

The Wild Swans at Coole

1 **Comparing ideas and themes**
Compare the memories of the speakers about a place in 'The Wild Swans at Coole' and 'Crossing the Loch'.

2 **Comparing writers' devices**
Compare the ways in which the writers of 'The Wild Swans at Coole' and 'Cold Knap Lake' use swans in the poems.

Spellbound

1 **Comparing ideas and themes**
Compare the feelings of the speakers in 'Spellbound' and 'The Prelude'.

2 **Comparing writers' devices**
Compare how the writers of 'Spellbound' and 'Storm in the Black Forest' use repetitions to show feelings.

Below the Green Corrie

1 **Comparing ideas and themes**
Compare the threats presented by the places in 'Below the Green Corrie' and 'Wind'.

2 **Comparing writers' devices**
Compare the ways in which the writers of 'Below the Green Corrie' and 'The Prelude' present mountains. Think about the ways they write about mountains.

Storm in the Black Forest

1 **Comparing ideas and themes**
Compare the violent weather in 'Storm in the Black Forest' and 'Wind'.

2 **Comparing writers' devices**
Compare the ways in which violent weather is presented in 'Storm in the Black Forest' and 'Wind' by the way the writers describe the weather.

Wind

1 **Comparing ideas and themes**
Compare the threats presented by nature in 'Wind' and 'The Prelude'.

2 **Comparing writers' devices**
Compare the ways in which the weather is presented in 'Wind' and 'Below the Green Corrie'.

My learning ▶

In this section you will learn how to:
- become familiar with the poems as a whole
- start to make links between the poems.

Getting to know the poems

Assessment Objectives:

 AO1 respond to texts critically and imaginatively; select and evaluate relevant textual detail to illustrate and support interpretations.

 AO2 explain how language, structure and form contribute to writers' presentation of ideas, themes and settings.

 AO3 make comparisons and explain links between texts, evaluating writers' different ways of expressing meaning and achieving effects.

The poems

Flag
John Agard

Out of the Blue (extract)
Simon Armitage

Mametz Wood
Owen Sheers

The Yellow Palm
Robert Minhinnick

The Right Word
Imtiaz Dharker

At the Border
Choman Hardi

Belfast Confetti
Ciaran Carson

Poppies
Jane Weir

Futility
Wilfred Owen

The Charge of the Light Brigade
Alfred, Lord Tennyson

Bayonet Charge
Ted Hughes

The Falling Leaves
Margaret Postgate Cole

Come On, Come Back
Stevie Smith

next to of course god america
e. e. cummings

Hawk Roosting
Ted Hughes

The poems in this chapter focus on conflict between countries and people, which produces violence and death. All the poems are in your AQA Anthology.

In this chapter you will be:

▶ looking at the individual poems

▶ comparing the poems

▶ learning how to approach exam questions.

This preparation will help you develop your writing skills in order to hit the Assessment Objectives. See page v for more information about what the Assessment Objectives mean. In the exam you will have to compare two poems from this chapter.

Getting started

The first thing to do is to get to know the 'Conflict' poems.

Read all the 'Conflict' poems in your AQA Anthology. Just notice what they seem to be about – don't worry about trying to make sense of every line.

Write the headings listed below on a sheet of paper. Under each heading make notes of any links between poems. Include poems that have similarities and differences. Use the tips below to help you.

Headings	Tips
What the poems are about	All the poems are about conflict – but what sort? If they belong to a particular war or time, which one? Does the attitude to conflict seem to be angry/regretful/accepting? Which poems seem to have similar attitudes?
Beginnings/endings	Find examples of lines that look similar, but where there's a difference too. For example, both 'Come On, Come Back' and 'The Charge of the Light Brigade' use repeated phrases at the end. How are they similar or different in effect?
Length	You might notice some distinct similarities or differences. Include the number and length of **stanzas**, if there are any.
Rhyme	Is there a regular **rhyme scheme**? Does it change? Be careful – some poems that don't seem to **rhyme** often use a lot of **half-rhyme** or **echoes**, like 'Futility', or might suddenly rhyme. Look at 'Mametz Wood', for example; there's a strong rhyme in the last three lines, but not before. If you were working on this poem, you'd need to think about why the writer does this.
Rhythm	Are there any poems with a strong **rhythm**, such as 'The Charge of the Light Brigade'? Are any of the others similar to this?
Language	Some poems make considerable use of repetition of words and phrases, but others hardly use repetition at all. Look for repetition in each poem. What effect does it have? If there is no repetition, why do you think the writer made that choice?
Imagery	Some poems are rich in **imagery**, such as **metaphors** and **similes**, while others might seem quite plain. Make a note of some obvious similarities and differences.

Now display your findings on a sheet of A3 in one of the following ways.

1   Spread the titles out on the sheet and draw links between them, labelling each one.

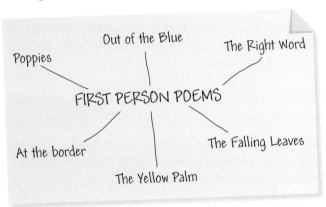

2   Draw a picture or symbol for each idea (such as death or nature) that appears in more than one poem, and group the poems around each – a poem can appear in more than one group.

3   Draw a picture, or pictures, for each poem on the sheet, and link similar ones with arrows.

In these activities you have started to tackle all three Assessment Objectives. Now you will be focusing on AO1 and AO2 as you look at the poems individually (pages 69–85). You will return to AO3 when you compare the poems (pages 86–89). Finally, you will look at how to turn your knowledge and skills into successful exam answers, before you attempt one yourself (pages 90–97).

Looking at the poems individually

Looking at the poems individually

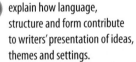

My learning ▶

In this section you will learn how to:
- develop your responses to the poems
- relate the Assessment Objectives to the poems.

This section of the chapter, pages 69–85, will lead you through each individual poem. Throughout, you will find examples of student responses at different levels.

In the exam, you will have to write about the poems individually. You will also have to compare two poems; one named poem and one unnamed poem, which means you can choose the second one.

Assessment Objectives:

The Assessment Objectives you will be focusing on in this part of the chapter are:

AO1 respond to texts critically and imaginatively; select and evaluate relevant textual detail to illustrate and support interpretations.

AO2 explain how language, structure and form contribute to writers' presentation of ideas, themes and settings.

Flag

by John Agard

Read the poem in your AQA Anthology, then complete the activities below.

GradeStudio

Sample answer C

To achieve a C on this AO1 descriptor, you need to show **sustained response to elements of text**. To do this, you need to write several connected comments about what you think about the poem. The following extract from a sample answer would hit the grade C requirement:

> Activity 2
> The flag stands for danger throughout. It's hugely dangerous right from the start as it 'brings a nation to its knees.' It encourages men to fight (which is dangerous) because it 'makes the guts of men grow bold' and 'dares the coward to relent'. The danger is made clear in the fourth stanza, because 'the blood you bleed' is what the flag will cause, and go on causing.

ACTIVITY 1

Initial responses

1 Why exactly is a flag an important 'piece of cloth' to write about? Find evidence from the poem to support your view.

2 Look at the first lines of each of the first four **stanzas**.
   a Identify the active words in these lines. For example, in line 1 of the first stanza the active word is 'fluttering'.
   b Why do you think Agard has chosen to make the flag seem like an active thing by doing this?

3 'Just a piece of cloth' is a small thing that actually has great power. Look at the last lines of the stanzas. How does the writer show the power of this piece of cloth?

4 Look at the last lines of each of the stanzas. How do they portray war?

5 Why would the **speaker's** 'friend' want 'such a cloth'? What does he think the flag might give him?

ACTIVITY 2

Words/phrases to explore (AO1)

Why do you think conscience has to be blinded 'to the end'? What might your conscience tell you not to do? Look at all the things that the flag is said to give in the poem.

Out of the Blue (extract)

by Simon Armitage

Read the poem in your AQA Anthology,
then complete the activities below.

Initial responses

ACTIVITY 1

1   What exactly is the man's situation in the poem?

2   The man in the building is waving a white shirt.
    What different things does he imagine the onlooker
    might see this as? Look at **stanzas** three and four.

3   There are lots of repetitions in this poem: of words,
    sentence forms and letters at the beginning of words
    (**alliteration**), like 'building burning'. Go through
    the poem and pick them all out. This will help you to
    notice where the patterns vary.

4   The man on the ledge is clearly desperate. Find
    places in the poem where you think that you can
    see or hear this. You could start with the **rhetorical
    question** at the end of the second stanza.

5   In the fourth stanza the heat of the flames is
    described as 'bullying, driving'. This is an example
    of **personification** (where something not human is
    given human characteristics).
    a   Why do you think the writer has chosen to do this?
    b   How does it make you feel the effect on the man
        on the ledge?

Words/phrases to explore (AO1 and AO2)

ACTIVITY 2

'My love' in the last line identifies the person the
character is speaking to for the first time.

1   Why does Armitage wait until this moment to
    mention this?

2   What effect does it have on the feeling of the poem
    as a whole? Try to suggest more than one point.

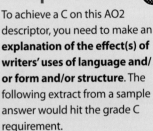

GradeStudio

Context

The poem refers to the people
who were trapped in the burning
twin towers in New York in the
9/11 attack, and who jumped to
their death from the buildings.

GradeStudio

Sample answer C

To achieve a C on this AO2
descriptor, you need to make an
**explanation of the effect(s) of
writers' uses of language and/
or form and/or structure**. The
following extract from a sample
answer would hit the grade C
requirement.

Activity I, question 3
In the second line of
the fifth stanza the
writer makes the word
'appalling' stand out by
repeating it, and putting
a full stop between the
two words before the
end of the line. It makes
the reader think about
what comes next, what is
'appalling', and in this
stanza it's 'Appalling' that
lots of other people are
falling to their deaths,
not just the speaker.

GradeStudio

Context

Mametz Wood In the First World War Battle of the Somme in July 1916, the 38th Welsh Division attacked the German positions in Mametz Wood. The wood was taken, but 4,000 Welsh troops perished.

▶ Poem Glossary

chit shoot, small piece

stands sentinel stands guard, like a sentry

dance-macabre a medieval idea of a dance of death, in which Death leads a row of dancing figures to the grave

GradeStudio

Sample answer ⓒ

To achieve a C on this AO2 descriptor, you need to make a make an **appropriate comment on ideas/themes**. The following extract from a sample answer would hit the grade C requirement.

> Activity I, question 6
> The earth, damaged by the war and the buried bodies, is gradually being restored. The farmers 'tended the land back into itself' and the earth is healing itself by slowly working the bones out onto the surface.

Mametz Wood

by Owen Sheers

Read the poem in your AQA Anthology, then complete the activities below.

Initial responses

ACTIVITY 1

1 Exactly what do farmers find in the field by Mametz Wood? List everything.

2 What happened to the soldiers? Look at the end of the third **stanza**.

3 What different times are mentioned in the poem?

4 How does Sheers make life seem fragile in the second stanza? Think about why he compares the skull to 'a blown and broken bird's egg'.

5 Why do you think Sheers describes the earth as 'standing sentinel'? What does it make the earth seem like?

6 Work out the idea that Sheers has about the earth in the fourth stanza. Think about what happens to a splinter in your finger.

7 In the last stanza, what do the skeletons appear to be doing? What effect does this have on the reader?

8 Find the **rhyme** in the last stanza. Why do you think Sheers uses rhyme here? Think which two words are connected by the rhyme.

Words/phrases to explore (AO1 and AO2)

ACTIVITY 2

The second line of the poem refers to 'the wasted young'. In the whole poem, how does the writer make you feel that they were 'wasted'? Write a paragraph about it beginning from that phrase.

The Yellow Palm

by Robert Minhinnick

Read the poem in your AQA Anthology, then complete the activities below.

Initial responses

ACTIVITY 1

1 The **speaker** in the poem sees lots of unhappiness and danger as he walks down the street. Make a list of what he sees.

2 Each of the first five **stanzas** contains a contrast of some sort. For example, the first stanza mentions 'lilac stems', and then the face of a man killed by poison gas. Find and write down the contrasts in the other stanzas.

3 In the third stanza, the speaker meets two beggars.
   a   What did these beggars used to be?
   b   How does the writer show the difference between what they were and what they are?

4 In the fourth stanza, even nature seems to be part of the war. How does the writer suggest this? Look for the words he uses as well as ideas.

5 In the fifth stanza, how is something dangerous made to seem not dangerous? Think about what it is compared to and the words used.

6 In the last stanza the beggar child is given something he hasn't asked for. What is it, and how does he get it? Think about what is happening in the previous stanza, and what falls out of the sky.

Words/phrases to explore (AO1 and AO2)

ACTIVITY 2

Do you think there are any signs of hope in the poem, or is it just bleak and depressing? Write a paragraph on this, supporting what you think with details from the poem. You could start with 'in a city such as this'.

GradeStudio

Sample answer ⓑ

To achieve a B on this AO2 descriptor, you need to show **thoughtful consideration of ideas/themes**. To do this, you need to think of more than one idea about the poem. The following extract from a sample answer would hit the grade B requirement.

> Activity 1, question 3
> The war has destroyed the soldiers' lives, making them into beggars; but this is made to seem sharper by the soldiers, who were not just guards but 'Imperial' Guards, being now blind, and ironically giving their soldiers' salutes in return for alms.

The Right Word

by Imtiaz Dharker

Read the poem in your AQA Anthology, then complete the activities below.

Initial responses

1 The woman in the poem is frightened of the figure outside. Why do you think she is frightened of him?

2 a Identify the different words used to describe the figure in the shadows, starting with 'terrorist'.
   b The word 'shadow' is repeated several times. Why do you think the writer does this?

3 Identify the different things the figure is doing in the shadows, beginning with 'lurking'.

4 The poem changes in the fifth **stanza**.
   a How does the first line of the stanza connect with 'a martyr'? Think about the use of the word 'God'.
   b How does the figure become clearer here, and more dangerous?

5 'No words can help me now.' What does this line show about how the **speaker** feels at this point?

6 Who do you think the 'you' might be at the beginning of the seventh stanza?

7 a How is the last stanza a surprise, after the rest of the poem? Think about the changes in the way the stanza is written as well as the change of feeling.
   b What is the effect of the last line?

▶ **Poem Glossary**

guerrilla warrior a member of an irregular armed force, not the official army

GradeStudio

Sample answer C

To achieve a C on this AO1 descriptor, you need to show **effective use of details.** The following extract from a sample answer would hit the grade C requirement:

Activity 1, question 7
The feeling of the poem changes in the last stanza to one of respect and civilised, peaceful behaviour. The invitation 'Come in' is repeated and the frightening figure actually 'steps in' and 'carefully' removes his shoes.

Words/phrases to explore (AO1)

Words are very important in this poem. What sort of person does the woman think the figure might be, and what does he turn out to be? Write some sentences about this, using details from the poem. Try to include the lines 'Are words no more/Than waving, wavering flags?'

At the Border

by Choman Hardi

Read the poem in your AQA Anthology, then complete the activities below.

Initial responses

1   What is the situation of the people waiting at the check-in point? Why do they think things will be different on the other side?

2   'It is your last check-in point in this country!' What do the words and punctuation suggest about the guard who says this line?

3   In lines 3–5, what is going to stay the same, and what will be different?

4   The two sides are divided by a 'thick iron chain'. Why do you think the writer uses the words 'thick' and 'iron'?

5   'The border guards told her off'. Look for all the mentions of the guards in the poem.

6   a   What do you think the writer wants you to think about the guards?
    b   What does this make you think about the authorities behind the guards?

7   What does the child think when she compares the two sides of the border? Look at the sixth **stanza**.

8   It is autumn, and it is raining on both sides of the border. Apart from being a literal description, what else might these two details say about the situation of the people in the poem? Will they be better or worse off on the other side of the border.

Words/phrases to explore (AO1 and AO2)

'The same chain of mountains encompassed all of us.' This is the fourth time in the poem that the word 'chain' is used. The meaning of 'chain' seems very different here from the 'thick iron chain'.

1   Could they be the same in any way?

2   How might both sides still be 'chained'?

GradeStudio

Sample answer

To achieve a D on this AO1 descriptor, you need to show **explained response to element(s) of text**. The following extract from a sample answer would hit the grade D requirement.

> Activity I, question 6a
> The guards in the poem seem repressive and harsh, because they shout at the refugees in the first line, and tell off the speaker's sister, who is only a child, just for putting her leg over the chain.

Belfast Confetti
by Ciaran Carson

Read the poem in your AQA Anthology, then complete the activities below.

Initial responses

1 List all the references you can find to weapons and ammunition in the poem.

2 What is ironic about the term 'Belfast confetti'? Think what occasion confetti is usually associated with, and what is happening in the poem.

3 To get into this poem, imagine a writer in the battle area trying to write. He uses punctuation marks as **metaphors** for the events and feelings that occur.
   a Why do you think the objects listed in line 2 are described as 'exclamation marks'? Remember what sort of feeling an exclamation mark usually shows.
   b Why is the explosion like an 'asterisk on the map'?
   c Why is the burst of rapid fire like 'a hyphenated line'? (Think about how you would draw bullets being fired.)
   d Why do you think the sentence 'kept stuttering'? Think of more than one reason here, if you can.

4 From lines 5–7, what do you think the **speaker** is trying to do and what is he feeling about his situation? Base your ideas on details in the text.

5 Line 8 lists items used by the troops. Why do you think the writer presents the troops like this, rather than saying 'The troops had …'? How does it make them appear to the reader? What does it show about the way the people in the city think about the troops?

GradeStudio

Sample answer E

To achieve an E on this AO1 descriptor, you need to show **supported response to text**. The following extract from a sample answer would hit the grade E requirement.

> Activity 2
> The man is confused at the end of the poem,
> 'Where am I going?'

To move to **explained response** in D, you would have to explain why he is confused, or what about.

Words/phrases to explore (AO1 and AO2)

'Dead end again'. How does the writer show that the speaker in the poem feels trapped? Starting from this phrase, write a couple of sentences on this.

Poppies

by Jane Weir

Read the poem in your AQA Anthology, then complete the activities below.

Initial responses

ACTIVITY 1

1 What does the mother do before her son leaves, and then after he leaves?

2 'Spasms of paper red, disrupting a blockade' describes the poppy on the blazer, but the writer uses words that make the reader think of war or injury. Find as many examples as you can of this technique in the rest of the poem.

3 In the second **stanza**, the **speaker** 'steeled the softening of her face'.
   a Why do you think her face softens, and why does she 'steel' it?
   b Why does the writer use the word 'steel'? What effect does it have?

4 Why do you think the mother finds her words 'slowly melting'? These words appear immediately after a pause. What effect does this pause have on the reader?

5 When the front door is opened, the world is 'overflowing like a treasure chest'. Why does this seem an unusual comparison in this poem? Do you think this is the mother's point of view or the son's?

6 Look at the last line. The mother hopes to hear 'your playground voice catching on the wind'. What is the effect of the last line on the reader? How many other references to the son's childhood can you find?

Words/phrases to explore (AO1 and AO2)

ACTIVITY 2

The writer describes herself leaning against the war memorial 'like a wishbone'. Find as many things to say about this comparison as you can. Think about what she looks like and what she is feeling.

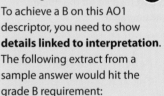

GradeStudio

Context

Armistice Day, when people remember those who have died fighting for their countries, is 11 November every year. Poppies are worn as a symbol of remembrance. In the poem, a mother is saying goodbye to her son, who is going away to war.

▶ **Poem Glossary**

bias binding   a strip of material often used for decoration round the edge of a piece of clothing

GradeStudio

Sample answer B

To achieve a B on this AO1 descriptor, you need to show **details linked to interpretation**. The following extract from a sample answer would hit the grade B requirement:

> Death is never far from the mother's thoughts. The information about the poppies being placed on graves that opens the poem has nothing to do with the son's departure, except for her fear, and when at the end of the poem the dove 'has led me' to the church yard and the war memorial, it has only led her here because they represent the death that she thinks about constantly, and fears.

Futility

by Wilfred Owen

Read the poem in your AQA Anthology, then complete the activities below.

GradeStudio

Sample answer Ⓓ

To achieve a D on this AO1 descriptor, you need to show **details used to support a range of comments**. The following extract from a sample answer would hit the grade D requirement.

> **Activity 1, question 2**
>
> The sun is very important in the poem. It used to 'rouse' the farmer in the mornings, not roughly but 'gently', and it is benevolent, 'the kind old sun'. It 'wakes the seeds' too, and brought life to 'the clays of a cold star'.

Initial responses

1 Look at line 3. What was the occupation of the dead soldier in peace time?

2 At the end of the first **stanza**, the sun is described as 'kind'. What other words in this stanza suggest that the sun is 'kind'?

3 The other adjective about the sun in that line is 'old'. How is the idea of the sun being 'old' used at the beginning of the second stanza?

4 There are three questions in the second stanza. Why does Owen choose to use questions here, do you think? What does he not understand?

5 The man's sides are 'still warm'. Look for the other references to warmth and cold in the poem, starting with the first line. Jot them down.

6 The sun once 'woke the clays of a cold star' and began life on our planet. What do you think the line beginning 'Was it for this' means? Remember what the **speaker** is looking at.

7 The poem is written in **half-rhyme** rather than full **rhyme**, as in 'seeds/sides': the consonants are the same, but the vowels change. Why do you think Owen has chosen this form for this poem about death? Think about the different sound this makes compared to a full rhyme.

Words/phrases to explore (AO1 and AO2)

The last line is about breaking sleep.

1 How is this idea used elsewhere in the poem, starting in line 2?

2 How is it a suitable ending for this poem, and what the speaker is saying?

The Charge of the Light Brigade

by Alfred, Lord Tennyson

Read the poem in your AQA Anthology, then complete the activities below.

Initial responses

1 What do the cavalrymen do during the course of the charge, and what happens to them? Be as exact as you can.

2 Read the first two lines out loud. How does Tennyson make the feeling of the charge on the horses come alive in these lines? Think about the use of repetition and **rhythm**.

3 All of the first five **stanzas** start with repeated words and phrases except one stanza.
   a Find this stanza.
   b Which line in this stanza suggests that going into battle is a huge mistake?

4 'Was there a man dismay'd?' suggests the courage of the soldiers. Where else in the poem can you find details that suggest courage?

5 In the third stanza, the men are surrounded. How do the first three lines of this stanza make you feel that the soldiers are surrounded?

6 How does the fifth stanza show the soldiers are returning? Find the exact words that tell you this.

7 Which words in the last stanza show the attitude that the poet thinks people should have about the soldiers?

Words/phrases to explore (AO1 and AO2)

'Some one had blundered'. Although the writer praises the soldiers who charge, what are the effects of the 'blunder' that 'some one' had made? Gather together the details from the poem that show the effects, and write a paragraph showing the effects of the mistake.

▶ **Poem Glossary**

volley'd bursts of simultaneous firing

battery smoke smoke created by firing from a group of guns or cannons

Cossack cavalry from the Ukraine

GradeStudio

Context

The charge took place at the Battle of Balaclava in 1854 against Russian forces. Due to mistakes in communication, over 600 cavalry charged into a valley defended by artillery. Nearly half of them were killed or wounded.

GradeStudio

Sample answer

To achieve a C on this AO2 descriptor, you need to show **explanation of the effect(s) of writers' uses of language and/or structure and/or form**. The following extract from a sample answer would hit the grade C requirement.

> The repetition of 'not' at the end of the fourth stanza is very striking, because it's the only time that the writer repeats a word like this, at the end of one line and the beginning of the next. 'Not' emphasises the loss – six hundred did not come back.

▶ Poem Glossary

Statuary a statue

Bayonet Charge

by Ted Hughes

Read the poem in your AQA Anthology, then complete the activities below.

Initial responses

ACTIVITY 1

1 Where is the soldier in the poem, what does he have, and what happens around him?

2 'Suddenly' sets off the active feeling of the whole poem. Beginning with 'running', find as many words of action in the poem as you can.

3 Hughes uses the senses a lot in this poem – seeing, hearing, smelling, tasting, touching.
   a Beginning with 'raw', find as many examples as you can of the senses being used.
   b What overall effect do you think this creates for the reader?

4 A lot of the **imagery** in the poem is violent, such as 'smacking the belly out of the air'. Find some more examples of violent imagery, and think what effect each of them has – more than one effect, if you can.

5 Before the action in the poem began, the soldier had a 'patriotic tear' in his eye. What happened to his feeling of patriotism, do you think? Find evidence from the poem for what you think.

6 a What is there about the 'yellow hare' which seems nightmarish?
   b What else in the poem seems to belong to a nightmare?

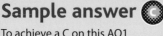

GradeStudio

Sample answer C

To achieve a C on this AO1 descriptor, you need to show **appropriate comment on ideas/ themes**. The following extract from a sample answer would hit the grade C requirement.

Activity 1, question 5

In the heat of the action, the soldier has no time for patriotic ideas. The 'patriotic tear' has turned to hot, dangerous metal, 'molten iron', like bullets, and 'King' and 'honour' have no value in the face of abject terror.

Words/phrases to explore (AO1 and AO2)

ACTIVITY 2

How is the soldier's 'terror' made clear? You could write a paragraph beginning with the last line of the poem, 'His terror's touchy dynamite'.

The Falling Leaves

by *Margaret Postgate Cole*

Read the poem in your AQA Anthology, then complete the activities below.

Initial responses

ACTIVITY 1

1 What does the **speaker** see as she rides, and what does it make her think of?

2 The last line of the poem tells you that the dead soldiers are being compared to snowflakes.
   a What else are the soldiers compared to in the poem?
   b Why do you think Cole compares them to these things? Think about what happens to leaves and snowflakes once they have fallen.

3 The leaves – and the soldiers, later – are described as 'brown' in the second line. Why, do you think?

4 The leaves fall 'thickly, silently'.
   a What does 'thickly' tell you about the leaves (the soldiers)?
   b What does the word 'silently' add to the feeling of what is going on?

5 The deaths of the soldiers are 'wiping out the noon'. Jot down as many reasons as you can for the writer's choice of these words. Think about the day, and the soldiers.

6 Who are the 'gallant multitude' in line 8? Why does the writer use the word 'multitude'?

7 Why do you think Cole describes the soldiers' 'beauty'? Compared to what? Think about the previous line.

Words/phrases to explore (AO1 and AO2)

ACTIVITY 2

The last word of the poem is 'clay', forming a **full rhyme** with 'lay', the only one in the poem. Why does the poet choose to use rhyme here and not elsewhere? Think about the two words that are joined together by the rhyme.

'Clay' means a type of earth. Look at the way the word is used in 'Futility', and it might add something to the meaning of this poem.

GradeStudio

Sample answer Ⓑ

To achieve a B on this AO1 descriptor, you need to show **details linked to interpretation**. The following extract from a sample answer would hit the grade B requirement.

> **Activity 1, question 4a**
> The importance of falling to the earth – like leaves and dying soldiers – is obvious from the title onwards. The leaves are 'dropping' to the earth 'thickly', showing the numbers involved as 'they fell', and 'falling' in the last line completes the circle begun with 'The Falling Leaves'.

Contexts

Austerlitz a famous battle in 1805 in the Napoleonic wars, though this poem is set at an unknown time in the future

Pan the Greek god of shepherds, who played pipes fashioned from reeds. He was a notorious seducer of nymphs. Kenneth Grahame refers to him in a chapter of *The Wind in the Willows* called 'The Piper at the Gates of Dawn'

▶ **Poem Glossary**

ominous suggesting that something unpleasant might happen

sentinel sentry

ebbing tide a tide receding, going away

Sample answer Ⓔ

To achieve an E on this AO2 descriptor, you need to show **awareness of writers' choice(s) of language and/or structure and/or form**. The following extract from a sample answer would hit the grade E requirement.

> **Activity 1, question 5**
> The writer uses three verbs quickly at the end of the line, 'strips, stands and lunges'.

To do better, there would have to be some indication of why the writer did this (D), or an explanation of it (C).

Come On, Come Back

by Stevie Smith

Read the poem in your AQA Anthology, then complete the activities below.

Initial responses

1   What has happened to Vaudevue, and what does she do?

2   Vaudevue's mind has been affected. How is this made clear in the first **stanza**? Think about what she is doing?

3   The reader is told at the beginning that this is 'an incident in a future war'. How does the writer suggest that this is happening in the future at the beginning of the second stanza?

4   The movement of the poem is quite uneven in the first three stanzas, but the two lines beginning 'The sand beneath' have a much livelier sound. Say them aloud to hear this.
    a   What makes them lively and even? Think about **rhythm** and **rhyme**, and how it is different from what has gone before.
    b   Why has Vaudevue now got a sense of purpose?

5   The pace is still quick at the beginning of the next stanza. Look at the first two lines, and decide how the writer makes this happen. Try to think of more than one thing.

6   The lake is described as 'adorable'. See if you can find other examples of Vaudevue loving the water. Why do you think she is attracted to it?

7   Look at the last stanza. What has happened to Vaudevue?

Words/phrases to explore (AO1)

Think about the effects of the last line, which is also the title. Do we want Vaudevue to 'come back' or are you happy for her?

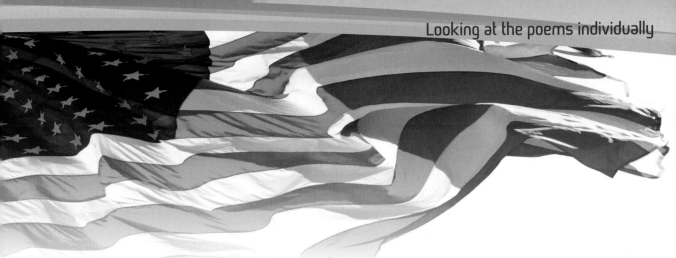

next to of course god america

by e. e. cummings

Read the poem in your AQA Anthology, then complete the activities below.

Initial responses

1 The **speaker** in the poem ('He spoke') seems to be in a rush. How does Cummings use **enjambment** (running the sense of one line on into the next) and punctuation to create this impression?

2 The speaker seems to be trying to make a patriotic speech. Does 'and so forth' help his case? What effect does it have, do you think?

3 What impression does 'we should worry' create of American attitudes to history?

4 The speaker says that America's 'sons acclaim' its glory using expressions such as 'by gee'. Why doesn't this seem right?

5 Why do you think the 'slaughter' is described as 'roaring'? What sort of picture does this create?

6 Think about lines 12 and 13. What sort of death did the 'heroic happy' die? What is the obvious answer to the question in line 13, even if it's not what the speaker intended?

Words/phrases to explore (AO1)

Think about the effect of the last line.

1 Why is it there? Were lines 1–13 the voice of the poet or someone else?

2 What is the writer's attitude to what the speaker says?

3 How do you know, exactly?

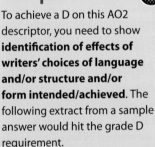

▶ **Poem Glossary**

acclaim praise

GradeStudio

Sample answer D

To achieve a D on this AO2 descriptor, you need to show **identification of effects of writers' choices of language and/or structure and/or form intended/achieved**. The following extract from a sample answer would hit the grade D requirement.

> **Activity 1, question 2**
> The writer keeps breaking off patriotic phrases like 'my country tis of', without putting 'thee' on the end, which makes the reader think it isn't patriotic at all.

This would have to be **explained** to get to C.

3 Conflict

Hawk Roosting

by Ted Hughes

Read the poem in your AQA Anthology, then complete the activities below.

▶ Poem Glossary

sophistry subtle reasoning or argument

GradeStudio

Sample answer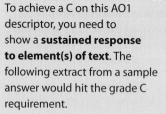

To achieve a C on this AO1 descriptor, you need to show a **sustained response to element(s) of text**. The following extract from a sample answer would hit the grade C requirement.

Activity 1, question 4

The hawk seems like a dictator as he sits in 'the top of the wood'. Everything seems to be working for him – the 'high trees', the air and the sun. Like a dictator, everything is below him, 'for my inspection'. 'No arguments assert my right' shows that he feels he can do anything without having to justify it.

ACTIVITY 1

Initial responses

1 What 'advantages' does the hawk have over everything it sees? Look through the whole poem for your answer, and jot the details down.

2 The first word of the poem is 'I'.
   a Underline all the examples you can find of 'I', 'me' or 'my' in the poem.
   b What does this tell you about the hawk's personality?

3 'I hold Creation in my foot'. Find as many examples as you can of the hawk's feeling of power in the poem.

4 If the hawk were human, what sort of person would he be? Kind? Generous? Something else? Think about your responses to questions 2 and 3.

5 Why might the hawk think that nature was made for him? Look at the second **stanza**.

6 Look at the first line of the third stanza. How does the writer make the hawk seem strong here? Listen to the sound of the words when you say them aloud.

7 'No arguments assert my right:'. What does assert the hawk's right? (Look at the last stanza.)

8 Each of the lines in the last stanza is **end-stopped** – it has a full stop at the end, forming a single sentence. Why does the writer do this, do you think? What final impression does it leave of the hawk?

ACTIVITY 2

Words/phrases to explore (AO1)

'Now I hold Creation in my foot'. How exactly is it true that he controls Creation? Think of as many reasons as you can, and write a paragraph about the hawk's control, beginning with this sentence from the poem.

Looking at the poems individually: what have you learned?

My learning ▶

In this section you will:
● think about which poems interested you most and why.

Complete Activities 1 and 2 below. As you do, think about which poems and which features of poems were most interesting to you.

Note that the words in bold in the tasks below refer to the key words in the Assessment Objectives.

Assessment Objective 1 (AO1)

ACTIVITY 1

1   Which of these poems did you **respond** to most strongly? You may have liked it, or disliked it, or found it the most interesting, or horrible. You may have a number of things to say about it.

Working with a partner, or by yourself, display your responses as a spider diagram, and then compare it with someone else's, to see if you have responded to the poems in similar ways.

2   Which poems did you find it easiest to offer an **interpretation** about? In other words, you had an opinion about a poem's meaning that you could argue from the text and **select detail** to support your opinion. For instance, you might have found it easy to argue and support the idea that 'The Charge of the Light Brigade' is a poem about bravery.

Suggesting more than one interpretation of a poem, or parts of a poem, gives you opportunities to score more marks. For instance, you could respond to the final stanza of 'The Yellow Palm' as either a life-giving moment or a moment of destruction.

Assessment Objective 2 (AO2)

ACTIVITY 2

1   Which features of **language**, **structure** or **form** did you understand best? The most promising ones to write about in the exam will be the ones where you have most to say. For instance, you might have found several things to say about:
   ● the effect of the repetitions of words in 'Flag' (**language**)
   ● the effects of language and stanza at the end of 'The Right Word' (**structure**)
   ● the effects of the rhymes in 'The Charge of the Light Brigade' (**form**).

2   What **ideas** did you pick out in the poems? Again, the best answers will probably identify more than one in a poem, or several aspects of one idea. For instance, you might have identified or explored more than one idea about war in 'The Charge of the Light Brigade.'

3 Conflict

My learning ▶

In this section you will learn how to:
- compare poems and address the Assessment Objectives
- develop writing skills and practise exam-style questions.

Comparing the 'Conflict' poems

Assessment Objective 3 is broken into two parts:

▶ comparing ideas and themes in the poems, with detail

▶ comparing the ways writers use language or structure or form, with detail.

In responding to the exam question, you will need to address both these parts.

Comparing ideas and themes

Read the poems 'The Falling Leaves' and 'Futility', then complete the activities below.

Assessment Objective:

The Assessment Objective you will be focusing on in this part of the chapter is:

 make comparisons and explain links between texts, evaluating writers' different ways of expressing meaning and achieving effects.

ACTIVITY 1

Think about the ideas and themes in the two poems.
List as many similarities and differences as you can. For example:
- Both poems are about the deaths of soldiers in war. Are the attitudes to death similar, or different?
- Both poems use nature a lot. What differences are there in the ways nature is used in each?

ACTIVITY 2

Using your list of similarities and differences from Activity 1, decide how different each of the poems are for each point you made.

For example, both of these poems are mourning the deaths of soldiers, but there are some differences in the ways the **speakers** seem to feel about the deaths. Think which words you would use to describe how they feel, and then find the words in the poems to support what you think. You could choose some of these words, for instance, and decide whether they apply to either of the poems, or to both of them: sad, angry, resigned, despairing, thoughtful.

Comparing writers' methods

Now you need to think about the similarities and differences in terms of the methods the writers use, and why they use them. Compare the differences in the ways the poems are written.

For these two poems you could consider the following questions:

▶ 'Futility' is written in two stanzas, but 'The Falling Leaves' is in one. Why do you think Owen decided to split the poem in this way, but Cole did not?

GradeStudio

Sample answer ⓔ

To achieve an E on this AO1 descriptor, you need to make a **supported response to the text**. The following extract from a sample answer would hit the grade E requirement.

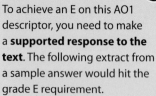

Activity 1
Both poems are about soldiers who have just been killed. At the beginning of 'Futility' it says 'Move him into the sun', so he probably died in the night, and in 'The Falling Leaves' she actually describes them 'dropping from their tree', which means she sees them die.

▶ Owen uses a mixture of **rhyme** and **half-rhyme** (like 'seeds' and 'sides') throughout the poem, whereas Cole doesn't use much rhyme. But what effects do these have? Look carefully at the rhymes at the end of the two poems – 'tall' and 'at all' in 'Futility' and 'lay' and 'clay' at the end of 'The Falling Leaves'. Why do each of the poets decide to connect those words at the end of their poems? What is the effect of the final word of each poem? Are the effects the same, or different?

▶ 'Futility' ends with three questions, but 'The Falling Leaves' does not have questions at all. Why? Think what each poet is saying, and what they feel about the deaths.

▶ Each stanza of 'Futility' begins with a command, 'Move' and 'Think'. 'The Falling Leaves' begins 'Today, as I rode by …'. How does this affect the feeling of each poem, do you think?

ACTIVITY 3

One of the best ways to score well in comparing poems is to compare two details, one from each poem, that you can say a lot about when you put them together. For example:

> Was it for this the clay grew tall?
> Oh what made fatuous sunbeams toil
> To break earth's sleep at all?

(Futility)

> Slain by no wind of age or pestilence,
> But in their beauty strewed
> Like snowflakes falling on the Flemish clay.

(The Falling Leaves)

You could say that both of these details use the word 'clay', but that would only be a simple link between poems, which is in the F band of marks. What more can you find to say? Think about the following points:

- Both of the poets are dealing with the deaths of soldiers, but they feel very differently about them. How do the differences come out in these lines, in what they say and the ways they are written?
- Choose one word from each piece that best shows what each poet feels.
- 'Clay' means slightly different things in the two poems. What, do you think? 'The Falling Leaves' is just about a specific place. How is this shown? How does the writer of the other poem show that he's thinking about something more than just this one death?
- The two endings feel very different when you read them aloud. What makes them so different? Think about the effects of the questions and exclamations in one poem, and the pictures created in the other.

You should have enough material now to write a good paragraph comparing the two details. Try it.

Putting it all together

To practise the skills you've been working on in these comparison activities, here are some more activities on a different pair of poems: 'Bayonet Charge' and 'The Charge of the Light Brigade'.

1 What ideas and themes can you find in the poems which are similar? What attitudes to war can you find in the poems? What similarities and differences are there in the physical details about the soldiers' experiences in battle? List as many similarities and differences as you can.

2 Now you have a list of similarities and differences between the two poems, you can discuss or jot down how similar they are, or how different. For instance, there is a lot of movement in both poems, but are they the same sort of movement? How different are they? All your responses need to be based on detail.

3 Now you need to compare how the poems are written. You could look at the following points:
   - How do the writers convey speed and action? Look at the **rhymes**, repetitions and verbs in 'Charge of the Light Brigade', and the verbs, lists and comparisons in 'Bayonet Charge'.
   - How do the poems end? Look at the last four lines of each, exploring similarities and differences between the ideas about honour in these lines, and how they are conveyed.

4 Now choose two details, one from each poem, that you think you could compare. For example:

> Flash'd all their sabres bare
> Flash'd as they turned in air
>
> (The Charge of the Light Brigade)

> He lugged a rifle numb as a smashed arm
>
> (Bayonet Charge)

The simple link between the two details is that they both describe the soldiers' weapons, but to reach the grades you are aiming for, you need to find as many similarities and differences as you can between the details.

So you would need to think about:
- What difference does the type of weapon make?
- How are the senses of seeing and feeling used differently?
- What different attitudes to the fight are suggested by the descriptions?
- How does each detail fit into the poems as a whole in what they reveal about the **speakers**?

Once you have chosen your two details, write a paragraph, or more, comparing the details.

GradeStudio

Sample answer

To achieve a C on this AO3 descriptor, you need to show **sustained focus on similarities/differences** with material for a range of comparisons. The following extract from a sample answer to Activity 4 would hit the grade C requirement.

The attitudes of the soldiers to the battles that they are in seem quite different. In 'The Charge of the Light Brigade' they seem courageous and strong, 'boldly they rode and well', whereas the soldier in 'Bayonet Charge' seems to act in panic, 'his sweat heavy' and 'In bewilderment'. The 'Light Brigade' soldiers seem determined as well, as 'Was there a man dismay'd?' suggests that they are not dismayed, whereas 'Bayonet Charge' mentions 'His terror's touchy dynamite'. The 'Light Brigade' soldiers seem to handle their weapons well, too.

'Flash'd all their sabres bare
Flash'd as they turned in air'

The repetition of 'flash'd' suggests that the way that the soldiers turned their swords in the light was strong and circular, which is why the sun flashes on them twice. 'He lugged a rifle numb as a smashed arm', though, suggests that he can hardly hold the weapon up in the air, which the sound of 'lugged' suggests, and that it is useless to him.

GradeStudio

Sample answer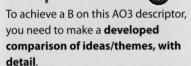

To achieve a B on this AO3 descriptor, you need to make a **developed comparison of ideas/themes, with detail**.

The following extract from a sample answer to the second task in Activity 4, question 3 would hit the grade B requirement.

'Honour' is an element in the ending of both poems, and in both is linked with nobility. 'King' is the first thing in the list in 'Bayonet Charge', and in 'Light Brigade' it is the soldiers themselves who are 'noble'. In 'Light Brigade', honour is a central idea, emphasised by its repetition at the beginning of succeeding lines, whereas in 'Bayonet Charge' it is only the second in a list, and only mentioned once. The list is to be 'dropped', though, because of the soldier's terror, whereas in 'Light Brigade' it is to be celebrated, which is emphasised by the exclamation marks at the end of the lines.

My learning

In this section you will learn how to:
● structure a response in the exam
● use the skills you have learned to perform successfully.

Assessment Objectives:

 AO1 respond to texts critically and imaginatively; select and evaluate relevant textual detail to illustrate and support interpretations.

 AO2 explain how language, structure and form contribute to writers' presentation of ideas, themes and settings.

 AO3 make comparisons and explain links between texts, evaluating writers' different ways of expressing meaning and achieving effects.

Writing in the exam

Writing your response – planning and structuring

Your process with any exam question should be.

Read

Read the questions – what exactly are you being asked to do? The questions should remind you about the Assessment Objectives. There will be a choice of two questions, so you need to make a choice quickly. Each question will ask you to compare a named poem with an unnamed poem, so your choice might be based on the poem that is named, or on what each question is asking you to do.

Think

This is the planning stage. The first word of the exam task is likely to be 'compare'. One of the descriptors in the mark band for a grade C is 'sustained focus on similarities/differences'. This suggests that a wise course of action would be to build your response around a comparison of the two poems.

This doesn't mean that everything you write should be comparative. You should decide how you're going to compare the poems before you write. Use a plan like the one on page 92. Within that, you need to jot down quickly some of the ideas from the poems, and perhaps one or two details that you're planning to use – you should choose things that you can write quite a lot about.

The thinking is more important than the writing here. The whole process might take 5 minutes, perhaps (certainly not less than 2 minutes). You only have 45 minutes for the whole task. Don't start writing straight away, think about the question carefully first!

Write

When you write, what you are going to show is:

▶ what you think about the poems

▶ why they are written in the ways that they are

▶ what happens when you compare the poems, or parts of them.

In other words, these are the things the Assessment Objectives focus on. The phrase 'or parts of them', is important. No question will ask you to write down everything you know about the poems; you have to select from what you know to think and write about the poems in answer to this question, in the ways that you've practised as you've worked through this section.

Edit

If you have any time left, you should look for ways to improve your answer. Don't look for spelling or punctuation errors: these don't carry marks here. Could you quickly add another possible meaning of a word or phrase that you've written about? Is there another idea about the effect of a writer's choice of language? Additions of this kind might gain you an extra mark.

Putting it into practice

Let's take a typical exam question:

Compare (AO3) the ways in which danger (AO1) is presented in 'Out of the Blue' and one other poem from 'Conflict' (AO2).

Let's suppose that you chose 'The Right Word' as a good poem to compare with 'Out of the Blue' – both show characters in dangerous situations, feeling afraid, and the poems are written very differently.

First, you need to jot down a few ideas from the poems that you're going to use when you write. For example:

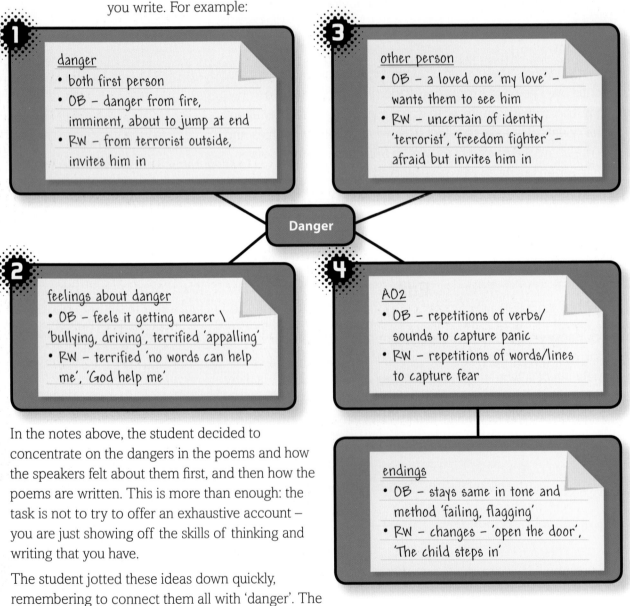

1

<u>danger</u>
- both first person
- OB – danger from fire, imminent, about to jump at end
- RW – from terrorist outside, invites him in

3

<u>other person</u>
- OB – a loved one 'my love' – wants them to see him
- RW – uncertain of identity 'terrorist', 'freedom fighter' – afraid but invites him in

Danger

2

<u>feelings about danger</u>
- OB – feels it getting nearer \ 'bullying, driving', terrified 'appalling'
- RW – terrified 'no words can help me', 'God help me'

4

<u>AO2</u>
- OB – repetitions of verbs/ sounds to capture panic
- RW – repetitions of words/lines to capture fear

<u>endings</u>
- OB – stays same in tone and method 'failing, flagging'
- RW – changes – 'open the door', 'The child steps in'

In the notes above, the student decided to concentrate on the dangers in the poems and how the speakers felt about them first, and then how the poems are written. This is more than enough: the task is not to try to offer an exhaustive account – you are just showing off the skills of thinking and writing that you have.

The student jotted these ideas down quickly, remembering to connect them all with 'danger'. The student decided that the endings would be a good choice to write a separate paragraph about.

GradeStudio

Read the extracts from these sample student answers, together with the question below and the examiner comments. You could then try the sample exam question on page 95.

Compare the ways that danger is presented in 'Out of the Blue' and one other poem from 'Conflict'.

Openings

 E grade answer

Student A

The speakers in 'Out of the Blue' and 'The Right Word' are both in danger which might kill them. In 'Out of the Blue' the man is in a 'building burning', and in 'The Right Word' there is a shadowy figure outside the speaker's house, and she is afraid that it might be a 'terrorist'.

Examiner comment

Student A successfully links the two poems by saying how serious the danger is, and supporting with detail from the poems. This means that there is **some comment on similarity** (E) with **support** (E).

 D grade answer

Student B

The speakers in 'Out of the Blue' and 'The Right Word' are both in danger. In 'Out of the Blue' the man is in a 'building burning', and in 'The Right Word' there is a shadowy figure outside the speaker's house, and she is afraid that it might be a 'terrorist'. She is not exactly sure what he is, though, because she calls him different things like 'a freedom-fighter' or a 'hostile militant'. The man in the other poem knows exactly what the danger is, because he can see the 'depth' in front of him, and feel 'the heat behind me'.

Examiner comment

Student B starts in the same way, but then builds on it so there is both an **explained response** (D) to the speaker in 'The Right Word', and some **structured comments on similarities and differences** (D) with **support** (D) when you look at the whole paragraph.

Examiner comment

Neither of the responses have yet begun to address AO2 (writers' methods). It is good that they have both started directly, not with something like 'In this essay I am going to write about...', which is a waste of time.

GradeStudio

A paragraph on Assessment Objective 1 A01

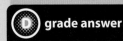

Student A

Both of the speakers are terrified of the dangers confronting them. The man in the building thinks the depth is 'appalling' and his 'nerves are sagging', as he sees other people 'wheeling, spiralling, falling' from the building. The woman in 'The Right Word' is also afraid, because outside there is a figure 'lurking in the shadows'. She is sure he is dangerous, whether he is a 'terrorist' or a 'freedom-fighter', and you can tell she is afraid by 'God help me' and 'no words can help me now'.

Examiner comment

In Student A's response, there is **some comment on similarity** (E) with **support** (E), as in the opening paragraph, and in addition there is some **awareness of feelings** (D) too.

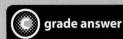

Student B

Both of the speakers are terrified of the dangers confronting them. The man in the building thinks the depth is 'appalling', and the feeling is emphasised by the repetition of the word after a full stop, so you have to stop and then say it again, 'Appalling'. He can see other people 'wind-milling, wheeling, spiralling, falling' from the building. All the 'ing' words get the sense of the movement turning and turning, and four times makes it as though he can't take his eyes off them. The woman in 'The Right Word' is also afraid, because outside there is a figure 'lurking in the shadows'. She is sure he is dangerous, whether he is a 'terrorist' or a 'freedom-fighter', and you can tell she is afraid by 'God help me' and 'no words can help me now'. She is not certain about him, though, and at the end she invites him into her house, and the child 'takes off his shoes', which suggests that the danger is over. The danger is not over for the man in the building, though. He is 'failing, flagging'.

Examiner comment

Student B takes the same overall idea, but adds more, so that there are two **explanations of effect** (C) on the first poem, simply by stopping and writing about the details chosen and how they work. There is also **structured comment on similarities/ differences** (D) with **support** (D), because the response adds another comparison at the end, going back to the first poem.

A paragraph on Assessment Objective 2 A02

 grade answer

Student A

Both poems use repetitions. 'Out of the Blue' repeats words like 'twirling' and 'turning' all the way through. 'The Right Word' repeats 'Outside' a lot.

Examiner comment

Student A achieves some comment on **similarity** (E) with **support** (E), and some awareness of a **writer at work** (E). Although a device (repetition) is identified, there is no sense of what it is for.

 grade answer

Student B

Both poems use repetitions. In 'Out of the Blue' the writer uses pairs and strings of words ending with 'ing', and often just with little twists like 'twirling, turning' to get a sense of the man's panic, and everything moving around him. Twice he repeats the same word, 'waving', which is then repeated again in the next line, to give a sense of desperation. The other word is 'appalling', which gives the idea of his fear, and the feeling is emphasised by the repetition of the word after a full stop, so you have to stop and then say it again, 'Appalling'. There's a line break straight after it, too, causing you to hang even longer over the word, as he looks down into the 'depth' underneath him.

Examiner comment

Student B's response does more than just **identify** (D) or **explain** (C) effect. There is only a **simple link** (F) at the beginning in terms of comparison, but in AO2 there are two **explanations of effect** (C), and then on 'Appalling' there is **appreciation of the writer's use of language** (B), and some **analysis** (A), which you would be credited with if you were entered for Higher Tier. The candidate achieves well by getting as much as possible out of one detail.

You are now ready to tackle an exam question. Here's one to try:

Compare how attitudes to conflict are presented in 'Flag' and one other poem from 'Conflict'.

When you've written your answer you could mark it, or get a partner to mark it, using the mark scheme on page 142.

Further comparison activities

Below are some comparison activities that you could attempt for each of the poems in the 'Character and voice' cluster.

Flag

1. **Comparing ideas and themes**
   Compare the attitudes of the voices to conflict in 'Flag' and 'Futility'.
2. **Comparing writers' devices**
   Compare the ways in which repeated words and phrases are used in 'Flag' and 'The Charge of the Light Brigade'.

Out of the Blue

1. **Comparing ideas and themes**
   Compare the ways in which the feelings of an individual in a desperate situation are shown in 'Out of the Blue' and 'Bayonet Charge'.
2. **Comparing writers' devices**
   Compare the ways in which danger is shown in 'Out of the Blue' and 'The Right Word'.

Mametz Wood

1. **Comparing ideas and themes**
   Compare the attitudes of the **speakers** to dead soldiers in 'Mametz Wood' and 'Futility'.
2. **Comparing writers' devices**
   Compare the ways in which death is presented in 'The Falling Leaves' and 'Mametz Wood'.

The Yellow Palm

1. **Comparing ideas and themes**
   Compare the effects of war on civilians in 'The Yellow Palm' and 'At the Border'.
2. **Comparing writers' devices**
   Compare how the writers of 'The Yellow Palm' and 'The Charge of the Light Brigade' make the cities seem horrible places.

The Right Word

1. **Comparing ideas and themes**
   Compare how the two sides of conflict are shown in 'The Right Word' and 'At the Border'.
2. **Comparing writers' devices**
   Compare the effects of the repetitions in 'The Right Word' and 'Flag'.

At the Border

1. **Comparing ideas and themes**
   Compare how feelings about a country are shown in 'At the Border' and 'Flag'.
2. **Comparing writers' devices**
   Compare the effects of the uses of the chain in 'At the Border' and the leaves in 'The Falling Leaves'.

Belfast Confetti

1. **Comparing ideas and themes**
   Compare how individual people caught up in war are shown in 'Belfast Confetti' and 'Bayonet Charge'.
2. **Comparing writers' devices**
   Compare the ways in which similes and metaphors are used in 'Belfast Confetti' and 'Bayonet Charge'.

Poppies

1. **Comparing ideas and themes**
   Compare the feelings shown by the speakers in 'Poppies' and 'At the Border'.
2. **Comparing writers' devices**
   Compare how feelings are shown in 'Poppies' and 'The Right Word'.

Futility

1 **Comparing ideas and themes**
   Compare the attitudes to death in war in 'Futility' and 'The Falling Leaves'.
2 **Comparing writers' devices**
   Compare the endings of 'Futility' and 'The Falling Leaves' – what effects they have, and how the writers make them work.

The Charge of the Light Brigade

1 **Comparing ideas and themes**
   Compare the attitudes to death in battle in 'The Charge of the Light Brigade' and 'Futility'.
2 **Comparing writers' devices**
   Compare the ways in which battle is shown in 'The Charge of the Light Brigade' and 'Bayonet Charge'.

Bayonet Charge

1 **Comparing ideas and themes**
   Compare the way conflict is presented in 'Bayonet Charge' and 'The Charge of the Light Brigade'.
2 **Comparing writers' devices**
   Compare the presentation of danger in 'Bayonet Charge' and 'The Charge of the Light Brigade'.

The Falling Leaves

1 **Comparing ideas and themes**
   Compare the attitudes to death in 'The Falling Leaves' and 'Futility'.
2 **Comparing writers' devices**
   Compare the ways in which the feelings of the poems are created in 'The Falling Leaves' and 'The Charge of the Light Brigade'.

Come On, Come Back

1 **Comparing ideas and themes**
   Compare the experiences of death in 'Come On, Come Back' and 'Out of the Blue'.
2 **Comparing writers' devices**
   Compare the ways in which an individual's experiences are shown in 'Come On, Come Back' and 'Bayonet Charge'.

next to of course god america

1 **Comparing ideas and themes**
   Compare the attitudes to death in 'next to of course god america' and 'The Charge of the Light Brigade'.
2 **Comparing writers' devices**
   Compare the ways in which the writers attack the idea of patriotism in 'next to of course god america' and 'Flag'.

Hawk Roosting

1 **Comparing ideas and themes**
   Compare the characters created in 'Hawk Roosting' and 'Bayonet Charge'.
2 **Comparing writers' devices**
   Compare the ways in which the writers of 'Hawk Roosting' and 'The Falling Leaves' present death by the ways they write.

My learning ▶

In this section you will learn how to:
● become familiar with the poems as a whole
● start to make links between the poems.

Getting to know the poems

The poems

The Manhunt *Simon Armitage*	**Brothers** *Andrew Forster*	**To His Coy Mistress** *Andrew Marvell*
Hour *Carol Ann Duffy*	**Praise Song for My Mother** *Grace Nichols*	**The Farmer's Bride** *Charlotte Mew*
In Paris with You *James Fenton*	**Harmonium** *Simon Armitage*	**Sister Maude** *Christina Rossetti*
Quickdraw *Carol Ann Duffy*	**Sonnet 116** *William Shakespeare*	**Nettles** *Vernon Scannell*
Ghazal *Mimi Khalvati*	**Sonnet 43** *Elizabeth Barrett Browning*	**Born Yesterday** *Philip Larkin*

The poems in this section focus on different types of relationships between people. All the poems are in your AQA Anthology.

In this chapter you will be:

▶ looking at the individual poems

▶ comparing the poems

▶ learning how to approach exam questions.

This preparation will help you develop your writing skills in order to hit the Assessment Objectives. See page v for more information about what the Assessment Objectives mean. In the exam you will have to compare two poems from this chapter.

Getting started

The first thing to do is to start to get to know the 'Relationships' poems.

ACTIVITY 1

Read all the 'Relationships' poems in your AQA Anthology. Just notice what they seem to be about – don't worry about trying to make sense of every line.

ACTIVITY 2

Write the headings listed below on a sheet of paper. Under each heading make notes of any links between poems. Include poems that have similarities and differences. Use the tips below to help you.

Headings	Tips
What the poems are about	All the poems are about relationships but there are different types of relationships here, and different feelings – attraction, uncertainty, anger, love, and so on. Which poems seem to have similar attitudes or types of relationship?
Beginnings/endings	Find examples of lines that look a bit similar, but where there's a difference too. For example, both 'Hour' and 'The Farmer's Bride' use repetitions at the end. How are they similar or different in effect?
Length	You might notice some distinct similarities or differences. Include the number and length of **stanzas**, if there are any.
Rhyme	You need to look a little more carefully now. Is there a regular **rhyme scheme**? Does it change? What is the effect of **rhyme** in the poem? It's very different in 'Sonnet 43' and 'In Paris with You', for example.
Rhythm	Are there any poems with a strong **rhythm**, or a sudden change in rhythm? Look at the change at the end of 'To His Coy Mistress', for example. Are any of the others similar to this?
Language	Some poems make considerable use of repetition of words and phrases, but others hardly use repetition at all. Look for repetition in each poem. What effect does it have? If there is no repetition, why do you think the writer made that choice?
Imagery	Some poems are rich in **imagery**, such as **metaphors** and **similes**, while others might seem quite plain. Make a note of some obvious similarities and differences.

Now display your findings on a sheet of A3 in one of the following ways.

1 Spread the titles out on the sheet and draw links between them, labelling each one.

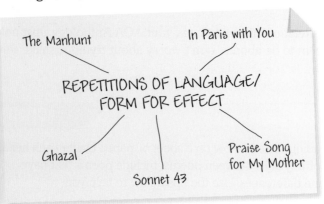

The Manhunt

In Paris with You

REPETITIONS OF LANGUAGE/ FORM FOR EFFECT

Ghazal

Sonnet 43

Praise Song for My Mother

2 Draw a picture or symbol for each idea (such as death or nature) that appears in more than one poem, and group the poems around each – a poem can appear in more than one group.

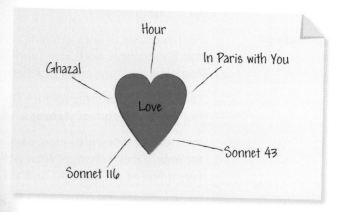

Hour

Ghazal

In Paris with You

Love

Sonnet 116

Sonnet 43

3 Draw a picture, or pictures, for each poem on the sheet, and link similar ones with arrows.

In these activities you have started to tackle all three Assessment Objectives. Now you will be focusing on AO1 and AO2 as you look at the poems individually (pages 101–117). You will return to AO3 when you compare the poems (pages 118–122). Finally, you will look at how to turn your knowledge and skills into successful exam answers, before you attempt one yourself (pages 123–129).

Looking at the poems individually

My learning ▷

In this section you will learn how to:
- develop your responses to the poems
- relate the Assessment Objectives to the poems.

This section of the chapter, pages 101–117, will lead you through each individual poem. Throughout, you will find examples of student responses at different levels.

In the exam, you will have to write about the poems individually. You will also have to compare two poems; one named poem and one unnamed poem, which means you can choose the second one.

Assessment Objectives:

The Assessment Objectives you will be focusing on in this part of the chapter are:

 respond to texts critically and imaginatively; select and evaluate relevant textual detail to illustrate and support interpretations.

 explain how language, structure and form contribute to writers' presentation of ideas, themes and settings.

The Manhunt
by Simon Armitage

Read the poem in your AQA Anthology, then complete the activities below.

GradeStudio

Examiner tip

Poetic devices
In the exam, you should refer to poetic devices, such as **metaphor** or **simile**, and other terms carefully and correctly. Terms in bold are explained in the Glossary of Poetic Devices (page 145).

Initial responses

ACTIVITY 1

1 a What different parts of the body does the **speaker** explore? Pick them out through the poem.
    b Is there anything you notice about the order in which they are explored?

2 There are a lot of word patterns here.
    a Pick out the verbs which describe what the speaker in the poem does. What picture do they give of her?
    b Trace the 'and…and' repetitions, starting with 'and handle and hold'. When do they end?
    c How do they add to the picture of what the speaker is doing?

GradeStudio

Sample answer ◉

To achieve a C on this AO2 descriptor, you need to show **explanation of effect of writer's uses of language and/or structure and/or form and effects on readers**. The following extract from a sample answer would hit the grade C requirement.

> Activity I, question 5
> The bullet is described as a 'foetus of metal' because it is buried within him, and it is also the beginning – like the birth – of his troubles.

3 Each part of the body (except one) is described with a **metaphor**. Find each one, starting with 'the frozen river', and decide if the metaphor is used to show you what something looks like, or something else.

4 The only part not to be described with a metaphor is the heart.
    a Why not, do you think?
    b The description of the heart is in the two shortest lines. Why do you think Armitage makes this choice?

5 Why do you think the bullet is described as a 'foetus'?

6 What do you think is the real source of the 'scarring', and why does the poet describe it as 'a sweating, unexploded mine'?

Words/phrases to explore (AO1 and AO2)

ACTIVITY 2

Why do you think the poem is called 'The Manhunt'? Think of as many reasons as you can and write them down.

Hour

by Carol Ann Duffy

Read the poem in your AQA Anthology, then complete the activities below.

Initial responses

1 The phrase 'Love's time's beggar' sets up ideas about time and money. Pick out all the words about time and all the words about money in the poem.

2 A single hour 'makes love rich'. What things in the second **stanza** are described in terms of wealth?

3 'Flowers' and 'wine' are associated with things given to lovers, but these lovers prefer something simpler. In the first and third stanzas, what simple things are as good as the usual things that lovers give to each other?

4 Find all the references to light in the poem. What sort of light is there?

5 The lovers seem to bribe ('backhanding') the night to come more slowly ('Time slows').
   a How do they do this?
   b What word implies that this takes a lot of doing?

6 Look at the last two lines. Why do you think Duffy picks out 'Now' as a single word, by putting full stops on each side of it?

Words/phrases to explore (AO1 and AO2)

ACTIVITY 2

In the fairy tale 'Rumpelstiltskin' gold is spun from straw.

1 How do the lovers spin gold (something worth a lot) from straw (something simple and cheap) in the whole poem?

2 Why do you think Duffy repeats the word 'gold' three times in the final line?

▶ **Poem Glossary**

Midas in Greek myth, Midas was a king who turned everything he touched into gold

cuckoo spit a froth left on plants by insects

Grade**Studio**

Sample answer D

To achieve a D on this AO1 descriptor, you need to give an **explained response to element(s) of text**. The following extract from a sample answer would hit the grade D requirement.

> Activity 1, question 1
> The lovers seem to be at the mercy of time, but they are not really, because they manage to slow time down, spending 'thousands of seconds' together, so that they make an hour 'shining', and time doesn't make love 'poor' at all.

In Paris with You

by James Fenton

Read the poem in your AQA Anthology, then complete the activities below.

Initial responses

ACTIVITY 1

1   How does the **speaker's** mood change during the poem? Find as many details from the poem as you can.

2   The speaker has had a bad experience in the past. Find all the clues you can in the first two **stanzas** to what has happened, and the way he feels about it. Start with 'I'm angry'.

3   Although the speaker appears to be angry, the **tone** (the feeling of the poem) is quite light.
    a   How does Fenton make the poem seem light?
    b   Look at the words he uses, and the **rhymes**.

4   Which word in the first stanza suggests that things might improve?

5   The poem sounds like somebody speaking. How does Fenton make the poem sound like this? Find some details to illustrate what you think.

6   The fourth stanza has the shortest lines in the poem. What signs are there in this stanza that the speaker's wounds are healing?

7   'Am I embarrassing you?' is the first question in the poem. Why do you think he uses one here? What does it show about the speaker?

GradeStudio

Sample answer B

To achieve a B on this AO1 descriptor, you need to show **details linked to interpretation**. The following extract from a sample answer would hit the grade B requirement.

> The speaker seems to wallow in his misery: 'tearful', 'resentful', and, tellingly, one of the 'talking wounded.' More evidence of this self-obsession is the fact that he rants to his partner throughout the poem, and only asks a question when he's clearly already in bed with her.

Words/phrases to explore (AO1 and AO2)

ACTIVITY 2

Compare the last stanza with the first.

1   How has the speaker changed?

2   How does Fenton show the changes by the ways he writes the stanzas?

Quickdraw
by Carol Ann Duffy

Read the poem in your AQA Anthology,
then complete the activities below.

Initial responses

ACTIVITY 1

1   How are the phones the two people use like guns? Use details from the poem to support your answer.

2   Look at the first word in the third line.
    a   What is the effect of placing it exactly here? Think about what it says about how the **speaker** feels.
    b   Which word does it **rhyme** with? (Look at the next line.)
    c   Why do you think the writer chose to rhyme these two words?

3   a   How might the voice be like 'a pellet in my ear'?
    b   What does that suggest about the state of the relationship between the two characters? Is it getting better or worse?

5   Look at the gunfighting **imagery** used in the second **stanza**.
    a   Which of the fighters is more successful?
    b   What do they succeed in doing?

6   Why is 'your kiss' described as 'silver bullets'? You may have to research what the phrase means.

7   a   What does each 'this' mean in the last line?
    b   How can it have two meanings?

Words/phrases to explore (AO1 and AO2)

ACTIVITY 2

How would you describe the state of the relationship in the poem? Write a paragraph about it. You could start with 'You've wounded me.'

Ghazal

by Mimi Khalvati

Read the poem in your AQA Anthology, then complete the activities below.

ACTIVITY 1

Initial responses

1 a What things does the **speaker** compare herself and her love to in the first **stanza**? Make a list.
   b What types of things are these?

2 a What type of things does she compare herself and her love to in the second stanza?
   b What is the effect of the **enjambment** here – the way that there is a line break between 'hang' and 'on', that makes a pause?

3 Look at stanzas three and four and the use of 'tattoo me'. How do you think the speaker would like the lover to behave here?

4 Look at stanzas five and six. The speaker uses some tree **imagery** here.
   a Why would she like to be 'bark'?
   b What does she want her lover to do?

5 a 'Marry' in the seventh stanza can mean 'match'. How would she like the two of them to be matched?
   b What different things would she like the lover to do?

6 How do the speaker's ideas get bigger in the last three stanzas? What does she compare herself and her lover to?

ACTIVITY 2

Words/phrases to explore (AO1)

How would you describe the attitude of the speaker to the other person in the poem? Clearly there is love in the poem, but which of the lovers is in control, do you think? Write a paragraph about the relationship, using details from the poem. You could start with 'subdue me'.

Brothers

by Andrew Forster

Read the poem in your AQA Anthology,
then complete the activities below.

Initial responses

1 **a** How does the writer show what the **speaker's** attitude to his brother is in the first line?

    b How has the writer chosen the word order to emphasise this?

2 In the first **stanza**, what don't the two older boys like about the young brother?

3 How is the attitude to the young brother shown again in the second stanza?

4 What does the word 'windmilled' suggest about the young boy?

5 The idea of a race runs right through the third stanza.

    a How does line 11 suggest that the two older boys are still children, really?

    b How does line 13 make you think of a race, and perhaps of the 'Olympic Gold'?

    c The speaker 'ran on'. What was he running towards, and what was he running away from at the same time?

    d What 'distance' has the speaker 'set in motion' between himself and his brother, do you think?

Words/phrases to explore (A01 and A02)

1 'Unable to close the distance I'd set in motion'. How has the speaker's attitude changed from the first line of the poem?

2 'In motion' suggests something moving. What do you think this might imply about the relationship between the speaker and his brother after the time when this incident took place?

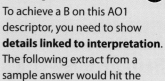

GradeStudio

Sample answer **B**

To achieve a B on this AO1 descriptor, you need to show **details linked to interpretation.** The following extract from a sample answer would hit the grade B requirement.

> Activity 2
> 'Grown-ups' are supposed to 'stroll the town', but the pace at the end tells of an older person's desperation about his relationship with his brother. He 'chased' and 'ran', but only towards failure. The 'hand' his brother reaches out does not reach him, and he is 'unable to close the distance' he has created.

Praise Song for My Mother

by Grace Nichols

Read the poem in your AQA Anthology, then complete the activities below.

▶ **Poem Glossary**

mantling covering

plantain a tropical food plant

ACTIVITY 1

Initial responses

1 In the poem the writer uses the senses to describe her mother – sight, smell, touch, taste and hearing. Find as many examples as you can of each of them, and write them down.

2 How is the mother like water, and the moon, and sunrise? Look at the last line of **stanzas** 1 to 3.

3 This short poem is full of patterns.
   a Look at the first three stanzas, and work out the repeated pattern. Think about the use of **metaphors** and adjectives.
   b Why do you think Nichols ends each one with a word ending 'ing'? How does it make you imagine the mother?

4 The stanza beginning at line 10 appears to break the pattern, but it's based on the same ideas.
   a What things are the same? Think about threes.
   b Why do you think the final word is repeated this time?
   c What is the effect on the poem of breaking the pattern in this way, do you think?

5 The last line is the only separate line. Why do you think Nichols does this? Think about the effect it has.

GradeStudio

Sample answer D

To achieve a D on this AO2 descriptor, you need to show **identification of effect of writer's choices of language and/or structure and/or form intended/achieved**. The following extract from a sample answer would hit the grade D requirement.

> **Activity 1, question 2**
> Nichols compares her mother to water and the moon and the sun, so you can see how important she was to her.

To get to C, the rather general statement above would have to be **explained**.

ACTIVITY 2

Words/phrases to explore (AO1 and AO2)

What is Nichols' attitude to her mother in the poem? Be as exact as you can – there are quite a few things you could say.

Harmonium

by Simon Armitage

Read the poem in your AQA Anthology,
then complete the activities below.

Initial responses

ACTIVITY 1

1 The **speaker** buys the old harmonium. What does it look like, and what happens to it?

2 The harmonium is 'gathering dust' and due to be 'bundled off to the skip'. Look through the poem for other references to things getting old or being disposed of.

3 How does Armitage **personify** (give human qualities to) the harmonium in lines 8 and 9? Think about which parts seem like human things.

4 The speaker can buy the harmonium 'for a song' and it 'struck a chord' with him.
   a How is the writer playing with words here?
   b What is it about the harmonium which attracts him?
      Look at the third **stanza** for a clue.

5 Look at the description of the speaker's father at the beginning of the last stanza. What is there here to remind you of the harmonium?

6 They carry the harmonium 'flat, laid on its back'. What, precisely, is the 'next box' that the father refers to?

7 a In the whole poem, how does Armitage connect the poem with the speaker's father?
   b What does that tell about how he feels about his father?
   c What effect does this have on you?

Words/phrases to explore (AO1 and AO2)

ACTIVITY 2

1 'too starved of breath to make itself heard.' Why can't the speaker say anything? Look at what his father has just said.

2 There is a lot of breath used in this poem – a harmonium uses air, pushed by the action of the treadles, to make the notes, and the father and son sing together in the third stanza. Why is it fitting that the poem ends in silence?

▶ **Poem Glossary**

Farrand Chapelette an old make of harmonium

beatify make sacred, make into saints

dottled stained with tobacco

harmonium an organ with foot pedals (**treadles**)

GradeStudio

Sample answer

To achieve a D on this AO2 descriptor, you need to show **awareness of ideas/themes**. The following extract from a sample answer would hit the grade D requirement.

> Activity 1, question 6
> The son is aware that his father is suggesting that he is nearing the end of his life, when he will be carried into the chapel in a box, meaning a coffin.

To get to C, you would have to be a lot more exact about the idea in the poem.

GradeStudio

Sample answer B

To achieve a B on this AO1 descriptor, you need to show **considered/qualified response to text**. The following extract from a sample answer would hit the grade B requirement.

Activity 2

The poem is full of definite statements about the unchangeable nature of love: it is 'never shaken', resistant to 'alteration', 'ever-fixéd.' But there is a moment of doubt: love's worth is 'unknown'.

Sonnet 116

by William Shakespeare

Read the poem in your AQA Anthology, then complete the activities below.

Initial responses

ACTIVITY 1

1 The poem suggests true love does not change with time. Which words in the first two lines suggest this?

2 'Love is not love' repeats the word 'love'. Where else in the next two lines does Shakespeare do this?

3 'Ever-fixéd' suggests something that cannot be moved by anything. How is this idea shown in the next three lines? Look at the **imagery** Shakespeare uses.

4 How is love not the 'fool' of Time? Think about what Shakespeare is saying about the nature of love.

5 a How does Shakespeare suggest in line 9 that young people are altered by time?
   b What does his 'sickle' do to them?

6 In lines 11 and 12, how is love made to seem everlasting?

7 Look at the last two lines. The **speaker** is very confident that true love does not change with time. How does Shakespeare make this seem final and definite? Think about how the lines are placed on the page and where **rhyme** is used.

Words/phrases to explore (AO1 and AO2)

ACTIVITY 2

In the whole poem, how is love seen as an 'ever-fixéd mark'? Think about each part of this phrase.

Sonnet 43

by Elizabeth Barrett Browning

Read the poem in your AQA Anthology,
then complete the activities below.

Initial responses

1 Count the number of ways in which the **speaker** loves 'thee'.

2 'the ends of Being and ideal Grace' describes a spiritual search. How does the whole sentence in lines 2–4 suggest something very large? Look at the way line 2 is written as well as what the words mean.

3 How do lines 5 and 6 suggest small things rather than large, but things for every time of day?

4 What has happened to the love that the speaker used to have for her 'lost saints'? Notice that she 'seemed' to lose it.

5 Look at the punctuation in lines 12 and 13. Dashes, commas and the exclamation mark have an effect on how you say and hear the line. What does it tell you about the speaker's feelings at this point? Remember that this is near to the end of her thoughts, too.

6 How is the final way she mentions how she loves 'thee' the biggest?

Words/phrases to explore (AO1 and AO2)

She will love him 'after death', 'if God choose'. This is a religious idea.

1 Where else in the poem does the poet use religious ideas? Look for words and phrases associated with religion.

2 What does this add to the poem, do you think? What sort of person is the speaker? Write a paragraph about the poem beginning, 'The speaker of the poem likes …'.

GradeStudio

Sample answer C

To achieve a C on this AO1 descriptor, you need to show **effective use of details to support interpretation**. The following extract from a sample answer would hit the grade C requirement.

The nature of the love the writer expresses changes at line 9. Up to that point the love seems quite spiritual – 'quiet' 'freely' 'purely' all suggest this – but now 'passion' appears.

To His Coy Mistress

by Andrew Marvell

Read the poem in your AQA Anthology, then complete the activities below.

GradeStudio

Sample answer C

To achieve a C on this AO2 descriptor, you need to show **explanation of effect of the writer's uses of language and/or structure and/or form and effects on readers**. The following extract from a sample answer would hit the grade C requirement.

Activity 1, question 6

The speaker describes the lovers (as he would like them to be) as being 'like am'rous birds of prey' in the third part. You might expect 'am'rous' birds to be gentle, like doves, but this idea suggests that he wants them to be strong and aggressive when they make love, which goes with 'tear our pleasures'. This is very physical love.

ACTIVITY 1

Initial responses

1   The three **stanzas** are like three stages of an argument, where the speaker is trying to get the woman to sleep with him. What are the stages? Look at the first line of each stanza, and particularly the first two words.

2   In the first stanza the **speaker** suggests what he would do if he had all the world and endless time. Find all the references you can to places and stretches of time. You could start with 'our long love's day'.

3   The speaker allots amounts of time to his mistress's body parts – for example, 'an hundred years' to the eyes.
    a   Find other examples in the poem of this?
    b   Why do you think he leaves the heart till 'the last age'?

4   The attitude to time changes in the second stanza. Why do you think Marvell describes time as having a 'wingèd chariot'?

5   a   Why does he describe eternity as a 'desert'? Remember what deserts are like, and what he is trying to persuade his mistress to do.
    b   What other words and phrases in the stanza suggest emptiness and death?

6   'Now' begins the third stanza. Look at the first seven lines, and find all the suggestions you can of 'now', and speed, and youth, and strength.

ACTIVITY 2

Words/phrases to explore (AO1 and AO2)

The last two lines complete the argument ('Thus, …').

1   What is the speaker saying about time here ('we cannot make …')?

2   What does the speaker think the lovers should do to 'make him run'?

You could write a paragraph showing how the whole poem leads up to these two lines.

The Farmer's Bride

by Charlotte Mew

Read the poem in your AQA Anthology, then complete the
activities below.

ACTIVITY 1

Initial responses

1   Work out the story of the poem – what happened in the past, the time
    of year now, and where the farmer and his bride are in the house?

2   What clues can you find in the first three lines to what goes wrong
    in the relationship? Think about the age of the woman.

3   The girl is described as running 'like a hare'.
    a   Find all the other comparisons you can between the girl and
        parts of nature, rather than 'all things human'.
    b   What evidence can you find that she is happier with animals
        than humans?

4   The last word of the second **stanza** is 'fast.', which means 'safely
    locked up' here. How is this word emphasised? Think about where it
    is placed and the punctuation?

5   The short fourth stanza describes the girl from the point of view of the
    man. What does it show about how he feels about her?

6   The fifth stanza describes the time of year. How could some of
    these details relate to the story of the girl and the farmer?

7   a   What do the repetitions in the last stanza show about what the
        speaker is thinking and feeling?
    b   What is the effect on the reader of ending the story like this, do
        you think?

ACTIVITY 2

Words/phrases to explore
(AO1 and AO2)

'Alone, poor maid.' How do you feel about
the girl's situation in the poem? What
difference does it make that the story is
narrated by the husband? You could write
a paragraph beginning with that phrase.

▶ **Poem Glossary**

fay   a fairy or elf

leveret   a young hare

rime   frost

GradeStudio

Sample answer **E**

To achieve an E on this AO1
descriptor, you need to show
**awareness of writer making
choice(s) of language and/or
structure and/or form**. The
following extract from a sample
answer would hit the grade E
requirement.

> Activity 1, question 3a
> The writer uses a simile
> to describe the girl, 'like
> a mouse'.

To improve on this, you would
have to **identify the effect** (D)
and **explain** it (C).

Sister Maude

by Christina Rossetti

Read the poem in your AQA Anthology, then complete the activities below.

GradeStudio

Sample answer ©

To achieve a C on this AO2 descriptor, you need to show **appropriate comment on ideas/themes**. The following extract from a sample answer would hit the grade C requirement.

> **Activity 1, question 2c**
> The depth of the speaker's hate for her sister is marked by her wish for Maude to suffer damnation, literally: where she and her parents, and of course her 'dear' might enter heaven, Maude must rest with 'death and sin' – in hell.

ACTIVITY 1

Initial responses

1   What has Maude done to her sister?

2   a   What words are used to describe Maude in the first **stanza**?
    b   What does this suggest about how the sister feels about Maude?
    c   What other things does she say in the rest of the poem that show how she feels about Maude?

3   The second stanza shows her love of her 'dear'. How can you tell that she regrets his death from the way the first line of the stanza is written?

4   Her 'dear' is dead, and so is her father. Her mother is described as being 'at Heaven-gate' which suggests she has recently died. How does this add to the effect of the story in the poem and how you feel about the **speaker**?

5   The speaker hopes that Maude will stay with 'death and sin'.
    a   What is she condemning her to?
    b   Why these two things? Think about the whole poem.

6   What features does the poem have which make it seem a bit like a spell? Research spells, and then look for:
    a   the threats and curses that the speaker makes
    b   the way the writer uses repetitions of words, phrases and sentence forms
    c   the way the writer uses **rhymes**.

ACTIVITY 2

Words/phrases to explore (A01)

What do you think of the speaker of the poem? Write a paragraph about her, using details from the poem to support your response.

Nettles

by *Vernon Scannell*

Read the poem in your AQA Anthology, then complete the activities below.

Initial responses

ACTIVITY 1

1 What happens to the boy in the poem? What does the father do?

2 The opening line is a simple statement. Find the other sentence which is like this one. Why does Scannell place them where he does?

3 Why does 'bed' seem to be a surprising name for where the nettles grow? Think about the possible contradiction here.

4 'Regiment' is the beginning of an extended **metaphor** comparing the nettles to an army.
  a Find all the other military terms in the poem.
  b Why is the use of military terms an appropriate idea to use for the nettles?

5 A metaphor like this is a way of getting over to the reader the **speaker's** emotions. Which word in line 3 does this more directly?

6 Why do you think the boy's grin is described as 'watery'?

7 'Not a nettle in that fierce parade/Stood upright.'
  Why is the parade 'fierce'?

8 What are the 'recruits' that have been called up?

9 How does the father feel in this poem? Suggest more than one feeling.

Words/phrases to explore (AO1 and AO2)

ACTIVITY 2

'My son would often feel sharp wounds again' is very general, compared to the specific first line.

1 How does 'wounds' continue the military metaphor?

2 What 'sharp wounds' might the son feel in the future, apart from nettle stings?

3 What does this reveal about the father's feelings and attitudes, do you think?

▶ **Poem Glossary**

billhook a gardening tool with a hooked blade

honed sharpened

pyre a fire built to burn a body as part of a funeral

GradeStudio

Sample answer

To achieve a D on this AO2 descriptor, you need to show **identification of effects of the writer's choices of language and/or structure and/or form intended/achieved**. The following extract from a sample answer would hit the grade D requirement.

> Activity 1, question 4b
> Comparing the nettles to 'green spears' makes them seem like something that will hurt the boy.

To move to C, the **effect** would have to be **explained** more clearly.

Born Yesterday
by Philip Larkin

Read the poem in your AQA Anthology, then complete the activities below.

▶ Poem Glossary

Born Yesterday the saying 'I wasn't born yesterday' means 'I'm not an innocent fool'

GradeStudio

Sample answer

To achieve a D on this AO2 descriptor, you need to show **explained response to elements(s) of text**. The following extract from a sample answer would hit the grade D requirement.

> **Activity 2**
> The speaker does not seem very sentimental. He doesn't seem to want the child to be 'beautiful' or to have love, but to be 'average', not 'ugly'. This seems to deny everything most people wish for newly born children.

To move to C, the response below would have to be extended, so that it became **sustained**.

ACTIVITY 1

Initial responses

1 In what ways is the baby like a 'tightly folded bud'? Think about what a bud is, and how it changes over time.

2 What is 'the usual stuff' that people wish for a baby, according to the **speaker**?

3 Find the first wish that the speaker makes for the child.
   a How does it sound like a wish? Notice where it comes in the poem, by counting the lines.
   b Why has the writer made the choice to put it there, do you think?

4 Why might unusual talents be a negative thing, according to the speaker?

5 Wishing for a child to be 'ordinary' and 'dull' may seem unusual, but look at the list of things in lines 21–23 which the speaker wishes for the child. What sort of qualities are these, do you think? Think how the words here are different to the words like 'innocence', 'love', 'ugly', 'good-looking.'

6 a Which word in the list is not downbeat like the rest of the poem, but actually sounds exciting?
   b How is the feeling it suggests carried into the final line?
   c What is the effect on the reader of finishing the poem like this, after the feeling of the earlier part of the poem?

ACTIVITY 2

Words/phrases to explore (AO1 and AO2)

What do the wishes for the child make you think about the speaker of the poem? Write a paragraph about what sort of person this is, using details from the poem.

Looking at the poems individually: what have you learned?

My learning

In this section you will:
- think about which poems interested you most and why.

Complete Activities 1 and 2 below. As you do these, think about which poems and which features of poems were most interesting to you.

Note that the words in bold in the tasks below refer to the key words in the Assessment Objectives.

Assessment Objective 1 (AO1)

ACTIVITY 1

1 Which of these poems did you **respond** to most strongly? You may have liked it, or disliked it, or found it the most interesting, or horrible. It might mean that you had a number of things to say about it.
Working with a partner, or by yourself, display your responses as a spider diagram, and then compare it with someone else's, to see if you have responded to the poems in similar ways.

2 Which poems did you find it easiest to offer an **interpretation** about? In other words, you had an opinion about a poem's meaning that you could argue from the text and **select detail** to support your opinion. For instance, you might have found it easy to argue and support the idea that the speaker in 'Praise Song for My Mother' admires her mother.
Suggesting more than one interpretation of a poem, or parts of a poem, gives you opportunities to score more marks. For instance, there are several ways you could interpret the nature of the speaker in 'The Farmer's Bride'.

Assessment Objective 2 (AO2)

ACTIVITY 2

1 Which features of **language**, **structure** or **form** did you understand best? The most promising ones to write about in the exam will be the ones where you have most to say. For instance, you might have found several things to say about:
- the effect of the heart not being represented through a metaphor in 'The Manhunt' (language).
- the gradual change in attitude in 'In Paris with You' (**structure**)
- the effects of the spaces between stanzas in 'Quickdraw' (**form**).

2 What **ideas** did you identify in the poems? Again, the best answers will probably identify several ideas in a poem, or several aspects of one idea. For instance, you might have identified or explored more than one idea about life in 'To His Coy Mistress'.

My learning ▶

In this section you will learn how to:
- compare poems and address the Assessment Objectives
- develop writing skills and practise exam-style questions.

Assessment Objective 3 is broken into two parts:

▶ comparing ideas and themes in the poems, with detail

▶ comparing the ways writers use language or structure or form, with detail.

In responding to the exam question, you will need to address both of these parts.

Comparing ideas and themes

Read 'In Paris with You' and 'Quickdraw' then complete the activities below.

Assessment Objective:

The Assessment Objective you will be focusing on in this part of the chapter is:

 make comparisons and explain links between texts, evaluating writers' different ways of expressing meaning and achieving effects.

ACTIVITY 1

Think about the ideas and themes in the two poems. List as many similarities and differences as you can. For example, both poems are about difficulties in love, so you could think about the following points:

1 Are the attitudes to the other people in the poems similar, or different? How?

2 Do the feelings of the characters in the poems change, or stay the same?

3 Which of these poems has stronger feelings for another person?

ACTIVITY 2

Using your list of similarities and differences from Activity 1, decide how different each of the poems are for each point you made. For example, both **speakers** have had difficulties with another person, but in 'In Paris with You' the difficulties seem to be over. The speaker in 'Quickdraw' seems to still be in the middle of her problems.

Use quotations or refer to the poem to support what you think.

GradeStudio

Sample answer

To achieve a grade E on this AO3 descriptor, you need to make **some comment(s) on similarities/differences, with detail**. The following extract from a sample answer to Activity 4 would hit the grade E requirement.

> Both characters feel like they are under attack. One thinks he is a 'hostage', so he's being held against his will, and the other feels she's being shot by her partner's voice.

Comparing writers' methods

Now you need to compare the differences in the ways the poems are written.

The two poems are very different in the ways they are written. They are both first person poems, though, and both speakers are 'wounded' – they both use this word.

- 'Quickdraw' uses lots of comparisons, and 'In Paris with You' does not. If you look at line 4 of 'In Paris with You', though, you'll find two comparisons. Now compare these with some of the comparisons in 'Quickdraw'. How do they work in the same way? Are they different?
- 'In Paris with You' uses lots of repetitions, but 'Quickdraw' does not. There are some repetitions in 'Quickdraw', though. What thoughts and situations are repeated?
- Compare the last **stanzas** of the two poems. They both use repetitions. How do the repetitions finish the poems off? Do they have different effects as endings on the reader. Which do you prefer, and why?

One of the best ways to score well in comparing poems is to compare two details, one from each poem, that you can say a lot about when you put them together. It doesn't matter whether you're comparing what the details are about, or the ways they're written, though if you're dealing with both it will provide more to say.

For instance, let's suppose that you chose these two details from these poems:

I'm a hostage. I'm maroonded.

(In Paris with You)

I'm all
Alone. You ring, quickdraw, your voice a pellet

(Quickdraw)

You could say that both of the characters feel that they are being attacked, but that would only be a simple link between the details, which is in the F band of marks. What more can you find to say? For example:

- Which of these details seems more serious? What is it that makes it more serious? Look at the choice of words as well as what they mean.
- Think about the choices Duffy has made in placing the word 'alone' exactly where it is. How has she isolated it, and why? Now compare the effect of this to the line from 'In Paris with You'. Is there a similar effect here, or not? If not, what effect does it have on the ways you think about the characters in the poems?
- 'I'm a hostage' and 'your voice a pellet' are both comparisons which make you aware of the other characters in the poems. How are the relationships in the poems different? Think first about these two details and what they suggest, and then about the whole poems.

You should have enough material now to write a good paragraph comparing the two details. Try it.

Sample answer D

To achieve a grade D on this AO3 descriptor, you need to make some **structured comments on similarities/ differences, with detail**. The following extract from a sample answer to Activity 4 would hit the grade D requirement.

> Both characters feel like they are under attack. One thinks he is a 'hostage', so he's being held against his will, and the other feels she's being shot by her partner's voice. The situations are not quite the same, though. The man in 'In Paris with You' is 'marooned' in Paris, but there's somebody with him that he falls for. The woman in 'Quickdraw' is 'alone', and stays alone and under attack right through the poem.

Putting it all together

To practise the skills you've been working on in these activities, here are some more activities on a different pair of poems: 'Praise Song for My Mother' and 'Ghazal.'

1 What ideas can you find in the poems which are similar? For example, both the **speakers** in the poems love the other person. What sort of relationships are these? Is the love in the two poems similar, or different?

2 How does each speaker depend on the other person in the poem, and what for? What does the other person in the poems give to the speakers?

3 Now you need to think about how the poems are written. You could say that one poem is written in two-line stanzas (couplets) and the other isn't, but that is only a simple link, which belongs in grade F, so you need to think a bit more.

- 'Ghazal' repeats 'If' throughout the poem, and 'Praise Song' repeats 'You were'. What does that say about the different relationships in the poems?
- Both poems use lots of comparisons between the characters in the poems and natural things, like leaves and water. Choose one or two similar ones and compare them, seeing if they have similar meanings and effects.
- Look at the endings of both poems – the last two lines of 'Ghazal' and the last line of 'Praise Song'. Both the poems end with large ideas. Is the ending of each poem written in the same way that the rest is written, or do they change? If there's a change, what is it, exactly? Looking at the shape of the poems on the page might help you to think about this.

Comparing writers' methods and purposes

ACTIVITY 6

Now choose two details, one from each poem, that you think you could compare. Let's suppose you chose these two:

> If I rise in the east as you die in the west,
> Die for my sake, my love, every night renew me

(Ghazal)

> You were
> sunrise to me
> rise and warm and streaming

(Praise Song for My Mother)

- Both of the details use the idea of sunrise. Which of these two is a simpler idea? Why do you think that is? Think about the different nature of the relationships.
- Why is one poem in the past tense, and not the other?
- What does each speaker receive, or want to receive, from the other person, do you think? You'll have to decide what 'renew me' might mean, and 'rise and warm and streaming'.

Now you could write a paragraph, or more, comparing the details.

Grade**Studio**

Sample answer

To achieve a C on this AO3 descriptor, you need to show **sustained focus on similarities/differences** with material for a range of comparisons. The following extract from a sample answer to Activity 6 would hit the grade C requirement.

Both speakers love the person that the poems are addressed to. They both think that the other person is huge in their lives, and think of them as the size of the sun, or the world: the daughter describes the mother as 'sunrise to me', and the lover describes her partner as 'heaven and earth to me', and as the dying sun: 'as you die in the west'. There is a difference though. The daughter knows that her mother was 'sunrise to me' because it has already happened, and the daughter is looking back on it. In 'Ghazal' it is something which is still happening, and might continue in the future. It is a more complicated love, because the speaker will only be renewed 'if'. 'If' implies some doubt, which does not exist in 'Praise Song'.

GradeStudio

Sample answer

To achieve a B on this AO3 descriptor, you need to show **developed comparison** with thoughtful selection of material for comparison. The following extract from a sample answer to Activity 6 would hit the grade B requirement, especially if it followed on from the paragraph on the previous page. The writing would have moved on from a sustained focus on one aspect of the poems, i.e. the damage to the characters, to another, developing the comparison.

> The daughter's feelings are much simpler than the lover's, actually. She admires her mother hugely, but simply and with no doubt. 'You were' is repeated four times, as this is all in the past, and completed, as 'Go to your wide futures' suggests. The relationship in 'Ghazal' does have some doubt, as the repetition of 'If' through the poem shows, and it is certainly not complete: 'If, when it ends'. Perhaps it has not even begun yet.

Writing in the exam

My learning ▶

In this section you will learn how to:
- structure a response in the exam
- use the skills you have learned to perform successfully.

Writing your response – planning and structuring

When faced with any exam question your approach should be:

Read

Read the questions and choose quickly which one to answer based on the poem that is named, or on what each question is asking you to do.

Think

This is the planning stage. The first word of the exam task is likely to be 'compare'. One of the descriptors in the mark band for a grade C is 'sustained focus on similarities/differences'. This suggests that a wise course of action would be to build your response around a comparison of the two poems.

This doesn't mean that everything you write should be comparative. You should decide how you're going to compare the poems before you write. Use a plan like the one on page 124. Within that, jot down ideas from the poems, and one or two details that you're planning to use. Choose things that you can write quite a lot about.

This whole process should take no more than 5 minutes (and not less than 2) as you only have 45 minutes for the whole task.

Write

When you write, you must show: what you think about the poems; why they are written in the ways they are; and what happens when you compare the poems, or parts of them (i.e. the things the Assessment Objectives focus on). The phrase 'or parts of them' is important. Don't write everything you know about the poems. Instead, select from what you know to write about the poems in a way that answers the question.

Edit

If you have any time left, you should look for ways to improve your answer. Could you add another meaning of a word or phrase? Is there another effect of a writer's choice of language? Additions of this kind might gain an extra mark.

Assessment Objectives:

 respond to texts critically and imaginatively; select and evaluate relevant textual detail to illustrate and support interpretations.

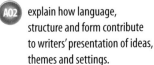 explain how language, structure and form contribute to writers' presentation of ideas, themes and settings.

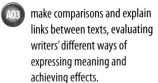 make comparisons and explain links between texts, evaluating writers' different ways of expressing meaning and achieving effects.

Putting it into practice

Let's take a typical exam question:

Compare (AO3) the ways that attitudes to another person (AO1) are presented in 'Nettles' and one other poem from 'Relationships' (AO2).

Let's suppose that you chose 'The Manhunt' as a good choice to compare with 'Nettles' – both are about a relationship with a person who has been damaged in some way, though the damage is very different in scale, and they both rely heavily on comparisons in the writing, with lots of use of military terms.

First, jot down a few ideas from the poems that you're going to use when you write. You could use the method shown below.

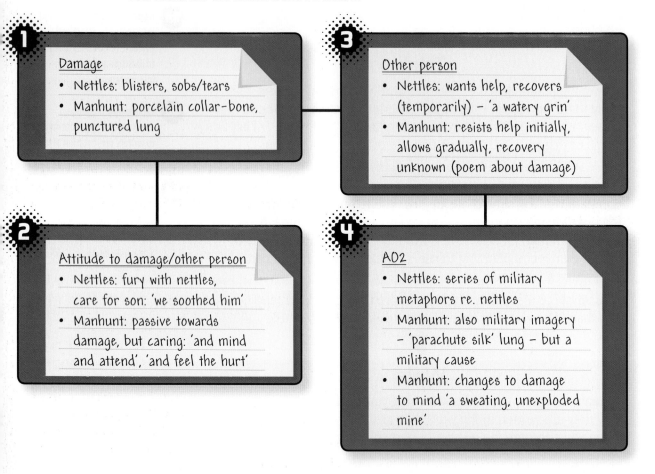

1

Damage
- Nettles: blisters, sobs/tears
- Manhunt: porcelain collar-bone, punctured lung

2

Attitude to damage/other person
- Nettles: fury with nettles, care for son: 'we soothed him'
- Manhunt: passive towards damage, but caring: 'and mind and attend', 'and feel the hurt'

3

Other person
- Nettles: wants help, recovers (temporarily) – 'a watery grin'
- Manhunt: resists help initially, allows gradually, recovery unknown (poem about damage)

4

AO2
- Nettles: series of military metaphors re. nettles
- Manhunt: also military imagery – 'parachute silk' lung – but a military cause
- Manhunt: changes to damage to mind 'a sweating, unexploded mine'

In the notes above, three ideas about the characters and attitudes in the poems have been identified, and one clear idea about the ways the poems are written, all of which can be compared. Some details to use have been jotted down. Of course, there are a lot more ideas you could think of, but the task is not to try to offer an exhaustive account – you are just showing off the skills of thinking and writing that you have, so four is plenty.

After thinking of the ideas, this student decided on the order that they should go in (shown by the numbers).

Read the extracts from these sample student answers, together with the question below and the examiner comments. You could then try the sample exam question on page 127.

Compare the ways in which attitudes to another person are presented in 'Nettles' and one other poem from 'Relationships'.

Openings

 E grade answer

Student A

Both poems are about people who have been hurt. The father in 'Nettles' is angry that his son has been hurt, because he 'slashed in fury' at the nettles that caused it. The speaker in 'The Manhunt' isn't so much angry as curious about what happened to her partner, because she talks about finding the 'source' of his pain. It's a long process, because it carries on right through the poem until the end, and even then it isn't over, because she only 'comes close' in the last line.

Examiner comment

Student A's response is scoring some marks already, because there is a **supported response** (E) about the father being angry, and a **comment on difference** with **material** (E). There is then an **explained response** (D) about the 'long process'. AO2 is not covered.

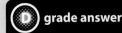 **D grade answer**

Student B

Both of the poems I have chosen are about damage to someone known to the speakers. The damage in 'Nettles' is fairly simple – a child has fallen into a nettle bed, and has 'blisters beaded on his tender skin'. The damage in 'The Manhunt' is a lot more serious, because the man has a scarred face, broken bones, and a 'punctured lung'. This damage seems very permanent, too, because the scarring will last and you don't know at the end whether he will recover or not, but in 'Nettles' the pain becomes 'not so raw' and he manages a smile. The worst pain for the wounded soldier seems to be 'deep in his mind'. The writer describes this as a 'sweating, unexploded mine' which makes you see how horrible the trauma is. 'Sweating' describes his feverish mind as well as his body, and the 'unexploded mine' suggests how fragile and dangerous his mental state is, if anybody takes a wrong step.

Examiner comment

Student B's response starts with some **structured comments on similarities/differences** (D), with **details for a range of comparisons** (D). This time there's an **effect identified** (D) about 'how horrible the trauma is', which is then **explained** (C) in the last sentence.

Examiner comment

Both students get on with the task straight away, without any need for a generalised opening paragraph.

A paragraph on Assessment Objective 1 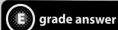 **A01**

E grade answer

Student A

> The speaker in 'Nettles' seems very emotional about his son, and what happens to him. He thinks the nettles act out of 'spite', and when he has 'soothed him' he goes outside and 'slashed with fury' at the nettles. 'The Manhunt' seems a lot gentler. You don't really know whether the speaker is angry or not, but what she does is 'mind and attend' him and 'feel the hurt' in his heart. The whole poem seems a lot quieter, because it's written in two line stanzas.

Examiner comment

Student A's paragraph has **supported responses** (E), and **some comment on difference** (E), **supported** (E). The last sentence shows **awareness of a writer at work** (E), but there is no **identified effect** (D).

D grade answer

Student B

> The speaker in 'Nettles' seems very emotional about his son, and what happens to him. He thinks the nettles act out of 'spite', and when he has 'soothed him' he goes outside and 'slashed with fury' at the nettles. 'The Manhunt' seems a lot gentler. You don't really know whether the speaker is angry or not, but what she does is 'mind and attend' him and 'feel the hurt' in his heart. You get the sense that she has to be very careful, because she has to 'trace' the line of his scar, which suggests being careful, and 'finger and thumb' the damage to the lung. She has to do it this way because 'he let me trace' and 'let me explore', so she feels very nervous about it. The writer describes his collar-bone as 'porcelain', which means she has to be careful because he is fragile.

Examiner comment

Student B's paragraph starts in the same way, but there is an **explained response** (D) to the idea of the speaker being careful, **awareness of feelings** (D), and an **effect identified** (D).

A paragraph on Assessment Objective 2

 grade answer

Student A

The writers of the poems use similar methods to describe things. They both use military comparisons. In 'Nettles' the nettles are described as a 'regiment of spite' and a 'fierce parade', and in 'The Manhunt' the punctured lung is described as 'parachute silk'.

Examiner comment

Student A has some **awareness of a writer at work** (E) twice, but in neither case does the student suggest what effect this might have. There is a **comment on comparison** with **material** (E).

 grade answer

Student B

The writers of the poems use similar methods, but they describe different things. They both use military comparisons. In 'Nettles' the nettles are described as a 'regiment of spite' and a 'fierce parade', and in 'The Manhunt' the punctured lung is described as 'parachute silk'. They are different, though, because the comparisons in 'Nettles' are used to describe the things that do the damage, and in 'The Manhunt' it's the actual damage that's described. The bullet lodged beneath his chest, for instance, is described as 'the foetus of metal'. 'Foetus' captures the physical idea of something within the body, but it also suggests something that may emerge, introducing the idea that recurs at the end of the poem of the 'unexploded mine' in the soldier's mind. 'Chest' and 'rest' form a rhyming couplet, too, which here suggest something at rest.

Examiner comment

Student B provides **structured comment on similarities and differences** (D). The **effect** of the 'foetus of metal' is **explained** (C), but then the response moves to the next band of AO2, providing **appreciation of the writer's uses of language and/or structure and/or form** (B) simply by finding more things to say about the detail and where it is placed in the poem.

You are now ready to tackle an exam question. Here's one to try:

Compare the ways that attitudes to another person are presented in 'Nettles' and one other poem from 'Relationships'.

When you've written your answer, you could mark it, or get a partner to mark it, using the mark scheme on page 142.

Further comparison activities

Below are some comparison activities that you could attempt for each of the poems in the 'Character and voice' cluster.

The Manhunt

1 **Comparing ideas and themes**
Compare the damage to the people described in 'The Manhunt' and 'Quickdraw'.

2 **Comparing writers' devices**
Compare the ways in which the writers of 'The Manhunt' and 'Hour' use the same sort of metaphors throughout the poems. What do they make you think about the people in the poems?

Hour

1 **Comparing ideas and themes**
Compare the ideas about love in 'Hour' and 'In Paris with You'.

2 **Comparing writers' devices**
Compare the ways in which the writers present love in 'Hour' and 'In Paris with You' by the ways they write about it.

In Paris with You

1 **Comparing ideas and themes**
Compare the attitudes of the speakers in 'In Paris with You' and 'To His Coy Mistress'.

2 **Comparing writers' devices**
Compare the ways in which the writers use repetitions in 'In Paris with You' and 'Praise Song for My Mother'.

Quickdraw

1 **Comparing ideas and themes**
Compare the relationships shown in 'Quickdraw' and 'In Paris with You'.

2 **Comparing writers' devices**
Compare the ways in which the writers use **metaphors** about fighting in 'Quickdraw' and 'The Manhunt'.

Ghazal

1 **Comparing ideas and themes**
Compare the feelings of the speakers shown in 'Ghazal' and 'Praise Song for My Mother'.

2 **Comparing writers' devices**
Compare the ways in which the writers present the feelings shown in 'Ghazal' and 'Praise Song for My Mother' by the ways they write about the other person.

Brothers

1 **Comparing ideas and themes**
Compare the feelings shown in 'Brothers' and 'Sister Maude'.

2 **Comparing writers' devices**
Compare the ways in which the writers present feelings in 'Brothers' and 'Sister Maude'.

Praise song for My Mother

1 **Comparing ideas and themes**
Compare the feelings of the **speakers** in 'Praise Song for My Mother' and 'Sonnet 43'.

2 **Comparing writers' devices**
Compare the ways in which the writers use repetitions to show how the characters feel in 'Praise Song for My Mother' and 'Sonnet 43'.

Harmonium

1 **Comparing ideas and themes**
Compare the feelings about parents in 'Praise Song for My Mother' and 'Harmonium'.

2 **Comparing writers' devices**
Compare the ways in which the writers show the feelings about parents in 'Praise Song for My Mother' and 'Harmonium' by the way they write about them.

Sonnet 116

1 **Comparing ideas and themes**
Compare the ideas about love shown in 'Sonnet 116' and 'Hour'.

2 **Comparing writers' devices**
Compare the ways in which the writers present love in 'Sonnet 116' and 'Hour' by the ways they write about it.

Sonnet 43

1 **Comparing ideas and themes**
Compare the feelings about a loved one shown in 'Sonnet 43' and 'Hour'.

2 **Comparing writers' devices**
Compare the ways in which love is shown in 'Sonnet 43' and 'In Paris with You'.

To His Coy Mistress

1 **Comparing ideas and themes**
Compare the attitudes to another person in 'To His Coy Mistress' and 'In Paris with You'.

2 **Comparing writers' devices**
Compare the ways in which the writers use comparisons drawn from nature to describe things in 'To His Coy Mistress' and 'Ghazal'.

The Farmer's Bride

1 **Comparing ideas and themes**
Compare the attitudes towards another person in 'The Farmer's Bride' and 'To His Coy Mistress'.

2 **Comparing writers' devices**
Compare the ways in which the writers end the poems in 'The Farmer's Bride' and 'To His Coy Mistress'.

Sister Maude

1 **Comparing ideas and themes**
Compare the state of mind of the speakers in 'Sister Maude' and 'In Paris with You'.

2 **Comparing writers' devices**
Compare the ways in which the writers use repetitions in 'Sister Maude' and 'In Paris with You'.

Nettles

1 **Comparing ideas and themes**
Compare the attitudes towards a child in 'Nettles' and 'Born Yesterday'.

2 **Comparing writers' devices**
Compare the ways in which the writers use metaphors in 'Nettles' and 'Quickdraw'.

Born Yesterday

1 **Comparing ideas and themes**
Compare the attitudes towards another person in 'Born Yesterday' and 'Praise Song for My Mother'.

2 **Comparing writers' devices**
Compare the ways in which the writers present what they have to say in 'Born Yesterday' and 'Praise Song for My Mother'.

My learning ▶

In this section you will learn how to:
- read an unseen poem
- annotate an unseen poem
- write successfully in the exam on the unseen poem.

What to look for when reading and annotating an unseen poem

Assessment Objectives:

 A01 respond to texts critically and imaginatively; select and evaluate relevant textual detail to illustrate and support interpretations.

 A02 explain how language, structure and form contribute to writers' presentation of ideas, themes and settings.

Introduction

Section B in the exam asks you to respond to an unseen poem – one that you have not prepared beforehand.

In this chapter of the book you will be:

▶ learning how to read the unseen poem in the exam

▶ learning how to annotate it before you write

▶ learning how to write successfully

▶ practising exam-style questions.

The skills you need to show are the same ones you worked on in thinking and writing about the poems you studied for Section A of the exam. The two Assessment Objectives tested are the same as those in Section A, so you should be familiar with these from the poems you have studied. You don't have to compare in Section B, so AO3 isn't present here. You have 30 minutes in the exam to answer the question on the unseen poem, and you have to think within this time before you start to write.

Reading the poem – what to look for

The Assessment Objectives ask you to do two things:

1 Say what you think the poem is about overall, what the poet has to say, and how these ideas and meanings are shown in the poem.

2 Say how the writer has written the poem to convey these ideas to the reader.

The two questions you will be asked about the poem are about exactly these things, so they are what you should look for when you read the poem.

Here is a list of questions to ask yourself as you read the unseen poem, which will help you to respond to the exam question.

1 What is this poem about as a whole, and what ideas are being expressed?

For example, the poem might be about a person, or a place, and might suggest ideas about the person or the place as the poem goes on. The ideas might grow as the poem unfolds, or just give some individual pictures. The poem might be about an event, and might have things to say about what happened.

2 How do the details of the poem create the ideas and meanings that you've found?

This might start with the title, and then be found in words, phrases and so on through the poem. If it is a descriptive poem, the writer might have used the senses in their writing. You don't have to write about every line of the poem in the exam, but you do have to use details from the poem to support what you say.

3 How does the writer use language to help get across what he or she has to say?

There's a whole range of devices which a writer might have used in writing the poem. You might find repetition, or figures of speech like **similes** or **metaphors**, or sounds like **alliteration**, or **assonance**, and so on. Whatever you find, remember that there is little point in just identifying it: you need to have an idea of why the writer is using a device.

4 How does the writer use structure to help get across what he or she has to say?

The writer might have built up the poem in stages towards the ending, or used different times like past and present, and so on.

5 How does the writer use form to help get across what he or she has to say?

The writer might have used **rhyme** or **rhythm** in a particular way, or spread words across lines (**enjambment**), or used a lot of **end-stopped lines** for a particular effect. Again, remember that the effect is what you have to think about. Just saying 'this poem uses rhyme,' for instance, would only get grade F.

6 What is your response to the poem?

When you have looked at the poem carefully you might well have a view about the poem – what you think about what is being said, and how successful you think the writing is. Don't be afraid to use this when you write – it's often a way of achieving higher marks.

Reading and annotating an unseen poem

Having read the guidance on the previous two pages on what to look for in an unseen poem, you are now going to put this into action in a particular poem.

Read the poem below several times, then complete Activity 1 opposite.

In Mrs Tilscher's Class

Carol Ann Duffy

You could travel up the Blue Nile
with your finger, tracing the route
while Mrs Tilscher chanted the scenery.
Tana. Ethiopia. Khartoum. Aswân.
That for an hour, then a skittle of milk
and the chalky Pyramids rubbed into dust.
A window opened with a long pole.
The laugh of a bell swung by a running child.

This was better than home. Enthralling books.
The classroom glowed like a sweet shop.
Sugar paper. Coloured shapes. Brady and Hindley
faded, like the faint, uneasy smudge of a mistake.
Mrs Tilscher loved you. Some mornings, you found
she'd left a good gold star by your name.
The scent of a pencil slowly, carefully, shaved.
A xylophone's nonsense heard from another form.

Over the Easter term, the inky tadpoles changed
from commas into exclamation marks. Three frogs
hopped in the playground, freed by a dunce,
followed by a line of kids, jumping and croaking
away from the lunch queue. A rough boy
told you how you were born. You kicked him, but stared
at your parents, appalled, when you got back home.

That feverish July, the air tasted of electricity.
A tangible alarm made you always untidy, hot,
fractious under the heavy, sexy sky. You asked her
how you were born and Mrs Tilscher smiled,
then turned away. Reports were handed out.
You ran through the gates, impatient to be grown,
as the sky split open into a thunderstorm.

Using the questions on pages 130 and 131 as a guide, list as many relevant points as you can find in the poem 'In Mrs Tilscher's Class'.

You could:
- start with what you think the poem is about
- then think about the way it's written.

Or you could do it the other way round, starting by noticing things like **rhyme** or **metaphors**.

Remember that you do need to do both these things to get as many marks as you can – saying what it's about without writing about methods is only half an answer, and writing about methods without showing what effects they have is only half an answer.

Possible answers

In the exam, as you find things, you should pick them out on the poem, by underlining, circling, or by making notes in the margin. How you do it is up to you, but these annotations will form the basis of what you are going to write. Here are some of the things you might have noticed in reading 'In Mrs Tilscher's Class'.

1 The title says a lot about the poem here – it is about education, in the sense that it's in a 'class', and 'Mrs Tilscher' is a primary-school teacher. There are a lot of details about the classroom, and about Mrs Tilscher, who was clearly admired by the child at the centre of the story. The poem seems to be about growing up, too – the child is 'impatient to be grown' at the end of the poem.

2 The child's love for Mrs Tilscher and her classroom is clear in the second stanza. Words here include 'better', 'enthralling', 'loved' and 'good'. The senses are used a lot in the last three lines – the appearance, smell and sound of the classroom. The second half has ideas about getting older, after the word 'changed'. Parents are seen in a different way, and the child is aware of it in the last stanza, as shown by the words 'feverish', 'sexy', 'impatient'. The last line seems to suggest a threatening change.

3 The **diction** of this poem – the type of words and phrases that are used – suggests a child's language, even though the point of view is of an adult looking back. 'You could travel', 'a good gold star'. The **imagery** describes childish enjoyment – 'the laugh of a bell', 'glowed like a sweet shop'.

4 The poem changes in the middle: the first two stanzas show enjoyment; the 'changed' in the first line of the third stanza marks a shift to uneasiness, then 'alarm'.

5 The key moment of the poem is emphasised by 'changed' at the end of a line – emphasised by the pause that follows.

If you had annotated this poem in the exam, this is what it might have looked like if you had seen the things listed on the previous page.

In Mrs Tilscher's Class

Children's point of view – 'you could': diction

You could travel up the Blue Nile
with your finger, tracing the route
while Mrs Tilscher chanted the scenery.
Tana. Ethiopia. Khartoum. Aswân.
That for an hour, then a skittle of milk
and the chalky Pyramids rubbed into dust.
A window opened with a long pole.

Metaphor/ enjoyment

The laugh of a bell swung by a running child.

This was better than home. Enthralling books.
The classroom glowed like a sweet shop. —— Simile – child's view
Sugar paper. Coloured shapes. Brady and Hindley

Safety

faded, like the faint, uneasy smudge of a mistake.
Mrs Tilscher loved you. Some mornings, you found
she'd left a good gold star by your name.

Senses: sight, smell, sound

The scent of a pencil slowly, carefully, shaved.
A xylophone's nonsense heard from another form.

Over the Easter term, the inky tadpoles changed —— End of line

Length

from commas into exclamation marks. Three frogs
hopped in the playground, freed by a dunce,
followed by a line of kids, jumping and croaking
away from the lunch queue. A rough boy
told you how you were born. You kicked him, but stared
at your parents, appalled, when you got back home.

That feverish July, the air tasted of electricity. —— Sense
A tangible alarm made you always untidy, hot,
fractious under the heavy, sexy sky. You asked her
how you were born and Mrs Tilscher smiled,

Suggests growing up

then turned away. Reports were handed out.—— End of year
You ran through the gates, impatient to be grown,
as the sky split open into a thunderstorm.

Threatening change

Writing a response in the exam

In this section you will learn:
- how to write successfully in the exam on the unseen poem
- what different levels of student response look like.

Writing in the exam

If 'In Mrs Tilscher's Class' appeared on the exam paper (which it won't!), the questions you might be asked to answer could be:

What does the poem say about the speaker's childhood experience?

How does the writer show what she thinks and feels?

You will have 30 minutes to do this whole task, so the examiner will not expect you to be writing a huge amount. Just like the poems you have to respond to in Section A, you are not expected to show that you understand every line of the poem, or to tell the 'story' of the whole thing by going through it from the beginning to the end. Instead, you have to use some details from the poem to show what skills you have learned about reading and writing about poetry, in line with the Assessment Objectives.

So, you can afford to spend 5–10 minutes thinking about what's on the page, and annotating it as shown opposite, so that you're ready to start writing. This will allow you to think about the poem as a whole before you start to write, instead of just starting to write about one particular feature of the poem.

For example, 'This poem is about a child's memory of primary school, but it is also about the disturbing changes that happen to a child at this age' would be a much better start than 'The writer uses metaphors like the laugh of a bell'.

You are left with 20–25 minutes to respond to the two questions, so concentrate on these and on using your annotations, though you might find more things to say as you write.

On the following two pages are sample student answers with examiner comments to the question on 'In Mrs Tilscher's Class' above. Read these, then have a go at a question on a new poem on the pages that follow.

GradeStudio

The poem these students have looked at is 'In Mrs Tilscher's Class' on page 132. The questions they are responding to is:

What does the poem say about the speaker's childhood experience?
How does the writer show what she thinks and feels?

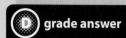 **grade answer**

Student A

> The speaker obviously loves the classroom, because she says it is 'enthralling' and 'like a sweet shop'. She likes her teacher too, because she says that she left 'a good gold star' by her name, and 'Mrs Tilscher loved you', so the child would love her back, probably, as children like to be loved. Her feelings don't stay exactly the same, though, because later on in the poem she seems to be growing up.
>
> The classroom is described as being 'like a sweet shop', so you can tell that the child really liked it. When the poem changes, the tadpoles changing from 'commas into exclamation marks' tells you that things are changing, and the 'sky split open into a thunderstorm' suggests it's not a good change.

- supported response
- explained response
- awareness of ideas/themes
- identification of effect
- range of comments

Examiner comment

Student A starts with a **supported response** (E) about the classroom, and then an **explained response** (D) about 'Mrs Tilscher loved you'. There's some **awareness of themes** (D) shown in the comment about growing up. In the second paragraph the student quickly **identifies the effect** (D) of 'like a sweet shop' without quite explaining it. She does this twice more, but as all three only identify rather than explaining, she doesn't achieve any more. The two paragraphs are marked together rather than separately, so by the end of the second paragraph she has also achieved **details used to support a range of comments** (D). All of the D criteria have been hit, but none of the C. If you look at the mark scheme on page 136 you'll see that this would be worth 12 marks (equivalent to a grade D).

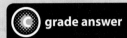

grade answer

Student B

The speaker obviously loves the classroom, because she says it is 'enthralling' and it 'glowed like a sweet shop'. She likes her teacher too, because she says that she left 'a good gold star' by her name, and 'Mrs Tilscher loved you', so the child would love her back, probably, as children like to be loved. 'The laugh of a bell' suggests it's a place of fun, and the books are 'enthralling' which tells you something about the character of the speaker, as she obviously liked reading and writing. Her feelings don't stay exactly the same, though, because later on in the poem she seems to be growing up. She is 'appalled' by what she hears about her parents, but 'impatient to be grown'.

The speaker says that the classroom 'Glowed like a sweet shop', so you can tell that the child really liked it. 'Glowed' suggests something that's shiny, which would attract her, and the idea of a 'sweet shop' is what a young child would like most. When the poem changes, the tadpoles changing from 'commas into exclamation marks' tells you that things are changing, and the 'sky split open into a thunderstorm' suggests it's not a good change. The weather seems to threaten all the way through the last stanza, and when it breaks at the end it's like the start of something new for the girl, the next stage of her life.

- supported response
- explained response
- range of comments
- sustained response
- effective use of details
- explanation of effect
- appropriate comment on meaning

Examiner comment

This response begins in the same way as the first one, but adds more comments with details, hitting a **range** (D), and a **sustained response** (C) to the speaker's feelings. There is **effective use of details** (C) to support the change in feelings. The second paragraph just adds two things to the writing by Student A, but very effectively. The effect of 'Glowed like a sweet shop' is **explained** (C) this time, and the last sentence gives an **appropriate comment on the idea** (C) in the last stanza. All of the C criteria have been hit. If you look at the mark scheme on page 144 you'll see that this would be worth 15 marks (equivalent to a grade C).

Here are two more poems for you to work on. You could do the first one with a partner, and try the second one on your own. You could mark both using the mark scheme on page 144.

mark both using the mark scheme on page 144.

ACTIVITY 2

Read the poem below, then complete the following questions.

1 **How has Cynddylan changed now that he has a tractor, and how does he feel about it?**

2 **How does the writer show Cynddylan's feelings by the way he writes?**

If you want to time yourself, in the exam you should spend around 30 minutes on this question.

GradeStudio

Context

This poem was written at about the time when tractors were replacing horses on farms for things like ploughing.

Cynddylan on a Tractor

R. S. Thomas

Ah, you should see Cynddylan on a tractor.
Gone the old look that yoked him to the soil,
He's a new man now, part of the machine,
His nerves of metal and his blood oil.
The clutch curses, but the gears obey
His least bidding, and lo, he's away
Out of the farmyard, scattering hens.
Riding to work now as a great man should,
He is the knight at arms breaking the fields'
Mirror of silence, emptying the wood
Of foxes and squirrels and bright jays.
The sun comes over the tall trees
Kindling all the hedges, but not for him
Who runs his engine on a different fuel.
And all the birds are singing, bills wide in vain,
As Cynddylan passes proudly up the lane.

Read the poem below, then complete the following questions.

1   How has the bus conductor been affected by his illness?

2   How does the writer show how the bus conductor feels by the ways he writes about him?

If you want to time yourself, in the exam you should spend around 30 minutes on this question.

My busconductor

Roger McGough

My busconductor tells me
he only has one kidney
and that may soon go on strike
through overwork.
Each busticket
takes on now a different shape
and texture.
He holds a ninepenny single
as if it were a rose
and puts the shilling in his bag
as a child into a gasmeter
His thin lips
have no quips
for fat factorygirls
and he ignores
the drunk who snores
and the oldman who talks to himself
and gets off at the wrong stop.
He goes gently to the bedroom
of the bus to collect
and watch familiar shops and pubs passby
(perhaps for the last time?)
The same old streets look different now
more distinct
as through new glasses.
And the sky
was it ever so blue?

And all the time
deepdown in the deserted busshelter of his mind
he thinks about his journey nearly done.
One day he'll clock on and never clock off
or clock off and never clock on.

Unit 2 Poetry across time – Sample Foundation Tier exam paper

---

Section A: Anthology

This section relates to the AQA Anthology that you have been using during the course.

Answer one question from this section on the poems you have studied in the Anthology.

You are advised to spend about 45 minutes on this section.

Relationships

EITHER

Question 1

Compare how children are presented in 'Nettles' and **one** other poem from 'Relationships'.

OR

Question 2

Compare how love is presented in 'Quickdraw' and **one** other poem from 'Relationships'.

Remember to compare: what the relationships in the poems are AND how the relationships are presented. *(36 marks)*

Conflict

EITHER

Question 3

Compare how the results of conflict are shown in 'The Falling Leaves' and **one** other poem from 'Conflict'.

OR

Question 4

Compare how feelings are presented in 'Bayonet Charge' and **one** other poem from 'Conflict'.

Remember to compare: the feelings in the poems AND how the feelings are presented. *(36 marks)*

Place

EITHER

Question 5

Compare how attitudes to a place are presented in 'Price We Pay for the Sun' and **one** other poem from 'Place'.

OR

Question 6

Compare how a dangerous place is presented in 'Cold Knap Lake' and **one** other poem from 'Place'.

Remember to compare: the places in the poems AND how the places are presented. *(36 marks)*

Character and voice

EITHER

Question 7

Compare how a character is presented in 'The Clown Punk' and **one** other poem from 'Character and voice'.

OR

Question 8

Compare how a character's attitude is presented in 'Below the Green Corrie' and **one** other poem from 'Character and voice'.

Remember to compare: the characters in the poems AND how the characters are presented.   *(36 marks)*

Section B: Unseen Poetry

Answer the question in this section.

You are advised to spend about 30 minutes on this section.

Read the poem below, and answer the question that follows.

Even Tho

Grace Nichols

Man I love
but won't let you devour
even though
I'm all watermelon
and starapple and plum
when you touch me
even tho
I'm all seamoss
and jellyfish
and tongue

Come
leh we go to de carnival

You be banana
I be avocado

Come
leh we hug up
and brace-up
and sweet one another up

But then
leh we break free
yes, leh we break free
And keep to de motion
of we own person/ality

Question 9

Answer both parts (a) and (b).

a   What are the speaker's feelings and attitudes about the man in the poem?

b   How does the writer present the feelings and attitudes in the poem?

(18 marks)

Mark schemes

Section A mark scheme

Below is the mark scheme for Section A of the Poetry unit.

(B) Mark Band 6 31–36 marks	**In response to the task, candidates demonstrate:** • considered/qualified response to text • details linked to interpretation • appreciation/consideration of writers' uses of language and/or structure and/or form and effects on readers • thoughtful consideration of ideas/themes • developed comparison in terms of ideas/themes, with detail • developed comparison in terms of writers' uses of language and/or structure and/or form and effects on readers, with detail	
(C) Mark Band 5 25–30 marks	**In response to the task, candidates demonstrate:** • sustained response to elements of text • effective use of details to support interpretation • explanation of effect(s) of writer's uses of language and/or structure and/or form and effects on readers • appropriate comment on ideas/themes • sustained focus on similarities/differences in terms of ideas/themes, with detail • sustained focus on similarities/differences in terms of writers' uses of language and/or structure and/or form, with detail	
(D) Mark Band 4 18–24 marks	**In response to the task, candidates demonstrate:** • explained response to element(s) of text • details used to support a range of comments • identification of effect(s) of writer's choices of language and/or structure and/or form intended/achieved • awareness of ideas/themes • structured comments on similarities/differences in terms of ideas/themes, with detail • structured comments on similarities/differences in terms of choices of language and/or structure and/or form intended/achieved, with detail	
(E) Mark Band 3 12–17 marks	**In response to the task, candidates demonstrate:** • supported response to text • details used to support points/comments • awareness of writer making choice(s) of language and/or structure and/or form • generalisation(s) about ideas/themes • some comments comparing ideas/themes, with detail • some comments comparing writers' choices of language and/or structure and/or form, with detail	
(F) Mark Band 2 6–11 marks	**In response to the task, candidates demonstrate:** • some clear responses • range of details used • simple identification of method(s) • some range of explicit meanings given • simple linkage in terms of idea(s)/theme(s) • simple linkage in terms of writers' methods	
(G) Mark Band 1 1–5 marks	**Candidates demonstrate:** • simple response(s) • familiarity with text/reference to some details • reference to writer's method(s) • simple comment on meaning(s) • linkage, perhaps implicit, re idea or theme • linkage, perhaps implicit, re method	
(U) 0 marks	Nothing worthy of credit	

This is exactly the mark scheme that examiners use. Below you will find what some of the terms mean, and how you use the scheme to get to a mark.

What do the words in the mark scheme mean?

F

▶ 'simple identification of method(s). This simply says that a method has been used, e.g. 'This poem rhymes'. To move to the next band an example has to be given.

▶ 'simple linkage' means a simple statement identifying a similarity or difference between the poems, for example 'both of these poems are about mountains'.

E

▶ 'supported response to text'. This is a response to the text supported with a detail or a quotation from the poem.

▶ 'some comments comparing' means isolated comments comparing, but not in a structured or sustained way.

D

▶ 'identification of effects'. This describes a comment that says what effect a particular device has, without explaining how it has that effect. Explaining would move it into Band 4.

▶ 'structured comments on similarities/differences' usually describes a passage comparing poems, or details from poems, in more than one way.

C

▶ 'sustained response to' describes a passage of writing about an element of the text, such as character or ideas, which covers several points. It could just be a paragraph rather than the whole response.

▶ Similarly, 'sustained focus on similarities/differences' describes a response which has comparison in mind all the time, though of course not every sentence has to be comparative.

B

▶ Some of the key words here are 'developed', 'considered/qualified' and 'consideration'. They all describe writing that deals with more than one thing, in the sense that one idea follows on or develops from another. 'It means this, but it could mean this as well, and it also implies that …'.

▶ A 'developed comparison' probably compares the poems, or details of the poems, but then goes on to compare them in another way that develops the first idea.

Examples of all of these terms can be found in the Examiner's comments accompanying the 'Grade Studio' sample answers.

Using the mark schemes

Using the mark schemes is quite simple, as the number of bullets in each band is the same as the number of marks that can be awarded. So, if a response hits all of the descriptors (bullets) in the 13–18 band and two of the 19–24 band, it is worth 20 marks. If it does one thing in a band above, though, say in the 25–30 band, that can count too. It goes in the place of one that's missing – so now the response gets 3 in the 19–24 band, and is worth 21 marks.

Section B mark scheme

This is the mark scheme the examiner will use to mark your answer to the Unseen Poetry task.

	In response to the task, candidates demonstrate:
B Mark Band 6 16–18 marks	• considered/qualified response to text • details linked to interpretation • appreciation/consideration of writer's uses of language and/or structure and/or form and effects on readers • thoughtful consideration of ideas/themes Information is presented in a way which assists with communication of meaning. Syntax and spelling are generally accurate.
C Mark Band 5 13-15 marks	• sustained response to elements of text • effective use of details to support interpretation • explanation of effect(s) of writer's uses of language and/or structure and/or form and effects on readers • appropriate comment on ideas/themes Information is usually presented in a way which assists with communication of meaning. Syntax and spelling are generally accurate.
D Mark Band 4 10-12 marks	• explained response to element(s) of text details used to support a range of comments • identification of effect(s) of writer's choices of language and/or structure and/or form intended/achieved • awareness of ideas/themes Information is presented in a way which is generally clear. Syntax and spelling have some degree of accuracy.
E Mark Band 3 7-9 marks	• supported response to text • details used to support points/comments • awareness of writer making choice(s) of language and/or structure and/or form • generalisation(s) about ideas/themes Despite lapses, information is presented in a way which is usually clear. Syntax and spelling have some degree of accuracy, although there are likely to be frequent errors.
F Mark Band 2 4-6 marks	• some clear responses • range of details used • simple identification of method(s) • some range of explicit meanings given Syntax and spelling are sufficiently clear to convey meaning
G Mark Band 1 1-3 marks	• simple response(s) • familiarity with text/reference to some details • reference to writer's method(s) • simple comment on meaning(s) Despite frequent lapses in syntax and spelling, meaning can be derived.
U 0 marks	Nothing worthy of credit

Glossary of Poetic Devices

alliteration   the deliberate repetition of consonant sounds at the beginning of words to gain a particular effect, e.g. 'and handle and hold' (The Manhunt)

assonance   the deliberate repetition of vowel sounds to gain a particular effect, e.g. 'tipples over' and 'spills down' (Storm in the Black Forest)

context   something outside the text that affects its meaning, such as:

▶ historical context, e.g. the Chernobyl incident in 'Neighbours'

▶ social context, e.g. nineteenth-century city conditions in 'London'

▶ language context, e.g. dialect in 'Hard Water', 'Singh Song'

dialect words   words from a particular region, e.g. 'mardy' (Hard Water)

diction   the choice of words used, e.g. formal or informal words

dramatic monologue   a poem supposedly spoken by a character, e.g. 'My Last Duchess'

end-stopped lines   lines of verse that end with a full stop, e.g. the last four lines of 'Hawk Roosting'

enjambment   the continuation of a sentence or phrase from one line into the next without a pause, e.g. 'and so forth oh/say can you see' (next to of course god america)

form   general way of organising a poem, e.g. rhyme, rhythm, etc. There are some particular forms such as ballads and sonnets

half-rhyme   words in which the consonants rhyme rather than the vowels, e.g. 'seeds/sides' (Futility)

imagery   language in a poem which conjures up an idea for the reader from one of the five senses. Specific forms of imagery include metaphors and similes

metaphor   an image which makes an implied comparison by stating that something is the thing it resembles, e.g. 'The tent of the hills' (Wind)

non-standard English   a variety of English other than standard, e.g. Caribbean English in 'Checking Out Me History'

personification   a device whereby an abstract concept or non-living thing is represented as having human characteristics, e.g. 'Old Father Time'

refrain   a recurring phrase or lines at the end of each verse of poetry, like a chorus, e.g. 'Brendon Gallacher' (Brendon Gallacher)

rhetorical question   a question to which no answer is expected

rhyme   the repetition of a vowel sound, usually in words at the end of lines, for example:
'I'm one of your talking wounded.
I'm a hostage. I'm maroonded.' (In Paris with You)
These can also be an internal rhyme, when a vowel sound is repeated within a line, such as 'rouse' and 'now' in this line from 'Futility':
'If anything might rouse him now'

rhyme scheme   the way rhymes within a poem are organised

rhyming couplets   two lines following one another which rhyme, e.g. 'word/heard' in the last two lines of 'Harmonium'

rhythm   the arrangement of words to form a regular beat through a pattern of stresses, e.g. 'The lone and level sands stretch far away' (Ozymandias)

simile   a comparison between two things, using 'like' or 'as', e.g. 'crowed like a rooster' (Cameo Appearance)

sonnet   a poem of fourteen lines, usually ending with a rhyming couplet, e.g. 'next to of course god america' (though this is a variation on a sonnet)

speaker   the 'voice' who is speaking in a poem written in the first person, e.g. the Duke in 'My Last Duchess'

stanza   a clearly demarcated part of a poem

structure   how the author has organised his/her work into patterns. Some fixed-form poems like sonnets have fixed structures of rhyme etc., but a poem might have structure in the way it is organised into stanzas, or what they open and close with, or where a particular word or idea is placed

symbol   something used to stand for or represent something else, e.g. the flag representing nationalism in 'Flag'

tone   the overall feeling or mood of a poem, e.g. the sorrowful tone of 'The Falling Leaves'

Heinemann is an imprint of Pearson Education Limited, a company incorporated in England and Wales, having its registered office at Edinburgh Gate, Harlow, Essex CM20 2JE. Registered company number: 872828

www.pearsonschoolsandfecolleges.co.uk

Heinemann is a registered trademark of Pearson Education Limited

Text © Pearson Education Limited

First published 2010

14 13 12 11 10
10 9 8 7 6 5 4 3 2 1

British Library Cataloguing in Publication Data

A catalogue record for this book is available from the British Library.

ISBN 978 0 435118 52 5

Designed and produced by Kamae Design, Oxford
Original illustrations © Pearson Education Limited 2010
Illustrated by Leo Brown and Kamae Design
Cover design by Wooden Ark Studios
Picture research by Sally Cole Picture Research
Cover photo © plainpicture/Readymade-Images
Printed and bound in Spain by Graficas Estella

Acknowledgements

The author and publisher would like to thank the following individuals and organisations for permission to reproduce photographs:

Michael Jenner/Corbis pp2, 14; Laurence Monneret/Stone/Getty Images pp5, 11; Bettmann/Corbis p6; 2002 Fotomas / Topham p7; Pernilla Zetterman/Etsa/Corbis p8; Louis Moses/zefa/Corbis p10; Steve J. Benbow. Getty Images p12; Mary Evans p13; Bronzino, Agnolo(1503–1572), school: portrait of Lucrezia di Cosimo 1.Florence, Galleria degli Uffizi© 1990. Photo Scala, Florence-courtesy of the Ministero Beni Att. Culturali p15; aida ricciardiello. Shutterstock p16; Robert Dowling/CORBIS p17; Hulton Archive/Getty Images p19; Carl Purcell/Corbis p20; Andrew Darrington/Alamy pp34, 38; Rob Matheson/Corbis pp36, 51; Richard Schultz/Corbis pp37, 47; Philippe Caron/Sygma/Corbis p39; Ashley Cooper/Corbis p40; Millais, John Everett 1829-1896. "Ophelia". 1852. (After Shakespeare, Hamlet). Oil on canvas, 76.2 x 111.8cm. London, Tate Gallery. AKG p41; Douglas Peebles/photolibrary group p42; PhotoSpin, Inc/Alamy p42; WIN-Initiative/Getty Images p44; Jack Andersen/Foodpix/Getty Images p45; Museum of London/HIP/TopFoto p46; AlaskaStock/Photolibrary group p48; Picavet/Getty images pp49, 53; Akg p50; Joanna McCarthy/Photolibrary p52; Kathy Collins/Getty Images pp66, 81; Hulton-Deutsch Collection/CORBIS p80; Gisela Delpho/Photolibrary pp69, 84; Benelux/Corbis p70; Sean Adair/Reuters p71; We are making a new World(1918), Paul Nash/Imperial War Museum. p72; 2006 Alinari/TopFoto pp73, 85; Radu Sighe/Reuters p75; Jeff J Mitchell UK/Reuters p76; Tim Cuff/Alamy p77; Tim Spence/Lightshaft Ltd/Photolibrary Group p78; Topham/Fotomas p79; YOSHITSUGU NISHIGAKI/amanaimages/Corbis p82; Jurgen Vogt/Alamy p83; Karin Smeds/Getty Images pp98, 115; Backhuysen, Ludolf 1631–1708. "Storm at a mountainous coast", c.1675. Oil on canvas, 173.5 x 341cm. Brussels, Musees Royaux des Beaux-Arts/AKG pp100,110; TMG. Getty Images pp101, 106; Jed Share/Getty Images p103; Roger-Viollet/Topfoto pp104, 117; Chris Cheadle/Photolibrary p105; J Richards/Alamy p107; Bob Thomas/Getty Images p108; Lars Dahlstrom/Getty Images p109; John Foley/Arcangel Images p111; Young Woman with Letter and Locket, 1667 (oil on panel) by Netscher, Caspar (1639–84) p112; Photolibrary Group p113; Hugh Shurley/Corbis p114; Mauro Fermariello/Photolibrary Group p116.

The author and publisher would like to thank the following individuals and organisations for permission to reproduce copyright material:

'Clown Punk' from *Tyrannosaurus Rex versus The Corduroy Kid* published by Faber and Faber; 'Checking Out Me History' © 1996 by John Agard reproduced by kind permission of John Agard c/o Caroline Sheldon Literary Agency Limited; 'Horse Whisperer' from *Fear of Thunder* by Andrew Forster, published by Flambard Press © Andrew Forster, 2007. Used by permission of Flambard Press; 'Medusa' from *The Worlds Wife* by Carol Ann Duffy, published by Picador. Used by permission of Picador, a division of Macmillan Books; 'Singh Song' from *Look We Have Coming to Dover* by Daljit Nagra, published by Faber and Faber; 'Brendon Gallacher' (25 lines) from *Two's Company* by Jackie Kay (Blackie, 1992) Copyright © Jackie Kay, 1992. Used by permission of Penguin Group (UK); 'Give' from *Dead Sea Poems* by Simon

Armitage, published by Faber and Faber; 'Les Grands Seigneurs' from *Hare Soup* by Dorothy Molloy published by Faber and Faber; 'The River God' from *New Selected Poems* published by New Direction Books. Used by permission of The Estate of James MacGibbon; 'The Hunchback in the Park' by Dylan Thomas from *The Poems* published by J.M. Dent. © Dylan Thomas. Granted by permission of David Higham Associates; 'The Ruined Main' artwork reproduced with permission of Punch Ltd, www.punch.co.uk; 'Case history: Alison (head injury)' by U A Fanthorpe, from *Collected Poems 1978-2003*, published by Perterloo Poets. © U A Fanthorpe. Used by permission of the Estate of U A Fanthorpe; 'On A Portrait of a Deaf Man' from *Best Loved Poems of John Betjeman* published by John Murray. Used by permission of John Murray and Aitken Alexander Associates; 'The Blackbird of Glanmore' from *District and Circle* by Seamus Heaney, published by Faber and Faber; 'A Vision' from *Tyrannosaurus Rex versus The Corduroy Kid* published by Faber and Faber; 'The Moment' by Margaret Atwood from *Eating Fire*, published by Virago, a division of Little Brown. Reproduced with permission of Curtis Brown Ltd. London on behalf of Margaret Atwood. © Margaret Atwood 1998; 'Cold Knap Lake' taken from *Collected Poems* by Gillian Clarke. © Gillian Clarke. Published by Carcanet Press Limited. Used by permission of Carcanet Press; 'Price We Pay for the Sun' from *The Fat Black Woman's Poems* published by Virago. © Grace Nichols, reproduced with permission of Curtis Brown Group Ltd.; 'Neighbours' taken from *Collected Poems* by Gillian Clarke. © Gillian Clarke. Published by Carcanet Press Limited. Used by permission of Carcanet Press; 'Crossing the Loch' from *Jizzen* by Kathleen Jamie. © 1999 Kathleen Jamie. Published by Picador. Used by permission of Picador, a division of Macmillan books; 'Hard Water' by Jean Sprackland © 2003. Published by Jonathan Cape. Used by permission of Random House UK; 'Below the Green Corrie' from *The Poems of Norman MacCaig* by Norman MacCaig is reproduced by permission of Polygon, an imprint of Birlinn Ltd. (www.birlinn.co.uk); 'Wind' from *Collected Poems* by Ted Hughes, published by Faber and Faber; 'Flag' from: *Half-Caste and other Poems* by John Agard © 2007. Published by Hodder Arnold; 'Out of the Blue' by Simon Armitage is reproduced from *Out of the Blue* (Enitharmon Press © 2008) Used by permission; 'Mametz Wood' from *Skirrid Hill* by Owen Sheers. First published by Seren Books. © 2005 Owen Sheers. Reproduced by permission of the author c/o Rogers, Coleridge & White Ltd., 20 Powis Mews, London, W11 1JN; 'The Yellow Palm' taken from Selected Poems by Robert Minhinnick. © Robert Minhinnick. Published by Carcanet Press Limited. Used by permission of Carcanet Press; 'The Right Word' taken from: *Terrorist at my Table* by Imtiaz Dharker. Published by Bloodaxe Books, © 2006. Used by permission; 'The Right Word' artwork reproduced with permission of Imtiaz Dha 'At the Border' taken from: *Life for Us* by Choman Hardi. Published by Bloodaxe Books © 2004. Used by permission; 'Belfast Confetti' by Ciaran Carson. Used by kind permission of the author and The Gallery Press, Loughcrew, Oldcastle, County Meath, Ireland from *Collected Poems* © 2008; 'Poppies' by Jane Weir. Used by kind permission of Templar Poetry; 'Bayonet Charge' from *Hawke in the Rain* by Ted Hughes, published by Faber and Faber; 'The Falling Leaves' by Margaret Postgate Cole, used by permission of David Higham Associates; 'Come On, Come Back' from *Not Waving but Drowning* by Stevie Smith published by Penguin Books. Used by permission of The Estate of James MacGibbon; 'next of course god america' Copyright 1926, 1954 © 1991 by the Trustees for the E.E. Cummings Trust. Copyright © 1985 by George James Firmage, from COMPLETE POEMS: 1904-1962 BY E.E. Cummings, edited by George J. Firmage. Used by permission of Liveright Publishing Corporation United States and WW Norton, United Kingdom; 'Hawk Roosting' from *Selected Poems* by Ted Hughes, published by Faber and Faber; 'The Manhunt' from *The Not Dead* by Simon Armitage, Published by Pomona Books. Used by permission; 'Hour' from *Rapture* by Carol Ann Duffy, published by Picador. Used by permission of Picador, a division of Macmillan Books; 'In Paris With You' by James Fenton from *Selected Poems* published by Penguin Books. Reprinted by permission of United Agents on behalf of James Fenton; 'Quickdraw' from *Rapture* by Carol Ann Duffy, published by Picador. Used by permission of Picador, a division of Macmillan Books; 'Ghazal' by Mimi Khalvati. Used by kind permission of the poet; 'Brothers' from *Fear of Thunder* by Andrew Forster, published by Flambard Press © Andrew Forster, 2007. Used by permission of Flambard Press; 'Praise Song for My Mother' from *The Fat Black Woman's Poems* published by Virago. © Grace Nichols, reproduced with permission of Curtis Brown Group Ltd.; 'Harmonium' by Simon Armitage © Simon Armitage. Used by permission of David Godwin Associates; 'Nettles' from *New and Collected Poems* by Vernon Scannell. Used by permission of The Estate of Vernon Scannell; 'Born Yesterday' by Philip Larkin, taken from *The Less Deceived* published by The Marvell Press; 'In Mrs Tilscher's Class' is taken from *The Other Country* by Carol Ann Duffy published by Anvil Press Poetry in 1990. © Carol Ann Duffy. Used by permission; 'Cynddylan on a Tractor' from Collected Poems 1945–1990 by RS Thomas, published by Phoenix, an imprint of the Orion Publishing Group, London. Used by permission; 'Even Tho' from Lazy Thoughts of a Lazy Woman by Grace Nichols, published by Virago. Copyright © Grace Nichols 1989, reproduced with permission of Curtis Brown Group Ltd.; 'My Bus Conductor' from The Mersey Sound by Roger McGough, published by Penguin Books Ltd. Used by permission of United Agents.

Every effort has been made to contact copyright holders of material reproduced in this book. Any omissions will be rectified in subsequent printings if notice is given to the publishers.